FLOWER CRAFT

FLOWER CRAFT

by BARBARA L. FARLIE and VIVIAN ABELL

DRAWINGS BY LYNNE FOY

The Bobbs-Merrill Company, Inc.
INDIANAPOLIS/NEW YORK

Designed by Helen Barrow
Photographs by Otto Maya
Manufactured in the United States of America
First printing

Library of Congress Cataloging in Publication Data
Farlie, Barbara L.
Flowercraft.
Includes index.
1. Artificial flowers.
I. Abell, Vivian, joint author.   II. Title.
TT890.F37   745.59′43   78-55664
ISBN 0-672-52150-4

To the late Evelyn Gendel,
for her editorial guidance and warm friendship

ACKNOWLEDGMENTS

We are grateful to the following individuals for their help on certain projects: Louise Anderson, Dorothy Brockel, Marla Jean Cassidy, Gerri Erikson, Pearl Freeman, Gloria Galbreath, Sherwood McCall, Margery Nicholson and Patricia Nimocks.

Contents

Introduction:
How Nice to Make Flowers

EVERYONE the world over loves flowers.

With flowers we can express love, give thanks, offer congratulations, welcome a baby, or wish someone happiness in a new home. Flowers are almost synonymous with such loving thoughts between friends.

Flowers also make an important decorating statement by giving shape, color and textural interest to a room; in fact, when used to the utmost effect, they tie a decorating scheme together not only in color but in period or style.

Unfortunately, most of us can enjoy fresh flowers for only a few months of the year, unless we are lucky enough to live in a warm climate, or have a greenhouse, or can afford to buy flowers every week during the long dreary months of winter. It was this sad state of affairs that got us interested in the art of making flowers—flowers that bloom in every room of our homes for 365 days a year.

A decade ago artificial flowers were frowned upon, and rightly so—most of those crude, garish blossoms were made of plastic and sold in five-and-ten stores. Today's artificial flowers—or permanent flowers, as we prefer to call them—are a vast improvement, thanks in part to flower-making techniques borrowed from the French. They are not only in chic good taste, but command fabulous prices in the best shops.

Learning how to make beautiful, permanent flowers is what this book is all about. If you have dreamed of luscious bouquets of silk or beaded flowers, you can make that dream come true by reading our how-to instructions and then going to work. The flowers we have designed for you range from real to fantasy, old-fashioned to contemporary, small to large, plain to exotic. Flowers that are meant to look real are composed of the finest fabrics. Others are made of paper, yarn, feathers and other unusual materials—these don't pretend to be real, but have loads of whimsical charm and are ideal for certain moods and locations.

Making flowers is not only great fun, but our approach places them within everyone's budget—they are yours for a modest financial outlay and a minimum of effort. Even if you insist you have two left hands when it comes to making things, we say you can make our flowers as easily as we can. We have spent years perfecting our patterns, so we know they work without benefit of any special skills or craft knowledge. One wonderful feature is that all our patterns are shown life-size; you don't have to scale up or enlarge them.

We feel our permanent flowers will appeal to just about everyone, young and old, no matter where they live. For example, this is a craft that will be a favorite of the apartment dweller who has no garden. Teachers and scout leaders will be delighted with the projects, many of which are simple enough for small fingers to manage. Likewise, chairpeople of bazaars and other fund-raising functions will be able to put volunteers to work making the flowers in this book—for decoration and for money-making projects.

There is no limit to where permanent flowers can be displayed. Best of all, they can add notes of distinction to your own home, notes that may be large and splashy, soft and elegant, amusing and fun—all to reflect your personality through your choice of flowers and the way you arrange them.

Be inventive with the permanent flowers around your house. For instance, we think they often look best when combined with plenty of greenery. This can take the form of real plants or cut foliage, or, what is more practical, artificial leaves purchased in a crafts store. They are quite realistic in appearance and surpass anything you can make yourself. They are inexpensive as well, and come in a wide range of styles and sizes.

Not since the Victorian era have people been as interested in plants as they are today. If you have a lot of potted plants in your house, we suggest tucking a few permanent flowers right into the soil to give them a new look—this is especially good when you need a centerpiece in a hurry for the dining table. When you are combining permanent flowers with real foliage from a florist, be sure to stick the foliage into Oasis with just a bit of water added from time to time; this will keep it from drying out so it will last several weeks.

Of course another kind of look that can be quite dramatic calls for flowers without any greenery at all. If filler flowers are needed, consider statice or baby's breath stuck into some Oasis to keep it fresh—or use filler flowers combined with small green velvet bows.

Change your arrangements of permanent flowers

often. If the same bouquet remains in a room for six months, you're not showing much imagination. You'll discover the sheer delight of putting the flowers in storage, bringing them out again several months later to combine with other flowers in a different way.

Keep your eyes open for flower containers, especially in antique shops and at flea markets. Containers are fun—and often inexpensive—to collect when traveling. Today it's possible to buy inexpensive reproductions of antique containers, but if you want to be even thriftier, here's your chance to use that cracked, chipped, or glued-together antique that you haven't been able to bring yourself to throw away. Other things to look out for are permanent flowers made during Victorian times; these are easy to find,

and while they may not be in mint condition, they can be used as patterns.

Once you have mastered the basic flower-making techniques, the sky's the limit. You'll be able to duplicate any flower you like by using a real flower as your pattern. The thing to keep in mind when creating your own pattern is: Simplify and strive for the overall effect—don't get bogged down in tiny details.

We hope our book will give you more than patterns and projects. Everyone has the desire to create something beautiful, and what is more beautiful than a flower? So, as you shape each petal, bud and blossom, we hope you'll take great pleasure in knowing that the flowers you're making will bloom for a long, long time.

PART I

GETTING READY

ONE:

Tools and Supplies

You will need very little equipment to make the flowers in this book. Many of the necessary items can be found around your house, while the rest can be purchased inexpensively in crafts, fabric, stationery, dime and grocery stores.

You probably have on hand the following tools and supplies: pair of sharp scissors; ball-point pen; felt-tip marking pen; ruler; wire cutters or pair of pliers with cutting edge; pad of tracing paper; cardboard; toothpicks; wax paper; aluminum foil; paper towel; string; serrated kitchen knife, can of spray starch; old nylon stockings or pantyhose; mixing bowls; empty glass jars with lids; ice pick or awl; straight pins; pair of manicure scissors; small handsaw.

In addition, you'll need the following items for many of the projects: compass; small artist's paintbrushes; acrylic and watercolor paints; white resin glue (Sobo); tacky glue (Velverette, Tube O' Tacky, Bond's 484); clear craft cement (Bond's 527); Mod Podge in matte finish; spray acrylic sealer (Mona Lisa Clear, Clear Cote, Krylon, or any crystal-clear brand); sponge brush or cosmetics sponge; styrofoam block; #28 green spool wire; #32 silver or gold spool wire; light green, dark green and brown floral tape; sizes #20 and #22 stem wires, uncovered and covered; assortment of artificial craft leaves, calyxes, stamens and peps (a pep is a large stamen).

For certain projects you'll need a few of the following supplies, but don't let the list scare you off—some are only called for in one project: fabrics such as silk, cotton and organza; ribbons and trims; crepe paper; commercial liquid dyes; colored oil pencils; liquid solder; instant papier-mâché; buttons; beads; #32 lacing wire; knitting needle; pinking shears; cotton or silk floss; velvet or plastic floral tubing; cotton cosmetics balls; dried sheet moss; floral adhesive; nonhardening floral clay; Oasis; floral picks.

Some of your flower-making materials are things you would normally discard, such as egg cartons, aluminum soft-drink cans and broken jewelry—so don't throw away anything while you're pursuing the delightful craft of flower-making. Other materials can be found for free in a natural setting—in the woods, around a marsh, or on the beach; some of these are pine cones, seedpods, grasses, thistleheads and seashells.

BUYING FABRIC

If you're making a number of flowers from the same pattern, it's more economical to buy fabric by the yard, or ribbon by the fifty-yard roll. Occasionally, for one or two flowers, one-eighth yard of fabric will be enough, but many stores won't sell such a small piece, and you'll have to buy one-fourth yard. However, once you start flower-making, you'll soon find use for extra scraps, so be sure to keep them.

Whenever you do a bit of redecorating involving patterned fabric or paper—curtains, bedspreads, wallpapers and so forth—consider purchasing extra amounts so you can make a matching floral arrangement. Coordinating flowers with your decorating fabrics can be a very smart decorating touch.

Stock up on fabrics and trims whenever your local fabric store has off-season sales.

WHERE TO BUY FLOWER PARTS

Keep a large assortment of leaves, calyxes and stamens on hand to avoid having to dash out to buy them for every single project. Although artificial greenery is inexpensive, you may as well save a few more pennies by stocking up when a local crafts store has a sale. When you don't have the exact size of leaf or calyx required for a specific project, simply cut down to size what you have on hand. If you have trouble locating flower parts, write one of the following companies for catalogs from which you can order the foliage you need:

Dennison's, Inc.
390 Fifth Avenue
New York, New York 10018

Designland Crafts
N. Ginsburg & Co.
112 North May Street
Chicago, Illinois 60607

Natcol Crafts, Inc.
Box 299
Redlands, California 92373

Every once in a while we resort to using artificial petals instead of making our own (see the Oriental Fruit Blossom on page 43 and the Tea Rose on page 102). The following firms carry lines of pre-cut and shaped petals sold in packages containing enough for a few flowers. They will also tell you which crafts stores in your area carry their petals:

Craft World
433 Hahn Road
Westminster, Maryland 21157

Hazel Pearson Handicrafts
4128 Temple City Boulevard
Rosemead, California 91770

Mangelsen's
Dept. PC-11 Box 3314
Omaha, Nebraska 68103

Natcol Crafts, Inc.
Box 299
Redlands, California 92373

Signaigo and Rossi, Inc.
9 Desbrosses Street
New York, New York 10013

Another alternative is the new Petal Maker Tool™, available from Natcol Crafts, Inc. This simple tool enables you to construct petals quickly and easily for fourteen different styles of fabric flowers.

In some stores ready-made craft stems for different types of flowers are also now available.

TWO:

Basic Flower-Making Techniques

Although each of the flowers in this book is different from the others, certain flower-making techniques (such as sizing of fabrics, applying floral tape to stems and so on) apply to many of them. So we are giving you the directions for the basic techniques right here—and you'll refer back to them as needed as you make your flowers. Once you've mastered a basic technique, go on to the next, and don't be afraid to give them all a try; if you follow our simple instructions, your initial efforts will turn out exceedingly well.

But first things first. Before you begin, take a minute to study Diagram A, which shows you a flower and its parts as they are referred to in this book.

MAKING YOUR PATTERNS

All patterns are shown exact size. There are two ways to reproduce the patterns for the projects in this book: with tracing paper or with cardboard.

TRACING PAPER

You'll use this when cutting fabric and paper and other soft materials: Lay a piece of tracing paper over the pattern in the book and trace the outline with a pencil or ball-point pen. Then cut out the tracing paper pattern with a sharp pair of scissors.

CARDBOARD

You'll use this on stiffer materials such as aluminum cans and hardened papier-mâché: First cut out a tracing paper pattern as directed above. Then place it on a piece of cardboard and draw around it with a pencil or ball-point pen. Cut out the cardboard pattern with an X-acto knife.

CUTTING OUT YOUR MATERIALS

SOFT MATERIALS

When cutting out fabric, paper and other soft materials, whenever possible fold the material carefully so you can cut several thicknesses at once. Then pin the tracing paper pattern in place on the material (just as you'd pin a sewing pattern) and simply cut around it.

When working with fabric, be sure to cut patterns on the bias—that is, pin the pattern so its length lines up with the cross/grain (bias) of the fabric. This helps prevent fraying when cutting. If the fabric frays anyway, go over the edges with a toothpick dipped in white resin glue to hold them firm.

STIFF MATERIALS

When cutting out stiff materials (aluminum cans, papier-mâché, etcetera), lay the cardboard pattern on the material and draw around it with a light pencil or with an empty ball-point pen. Then use your scissors and cut, following the outline.

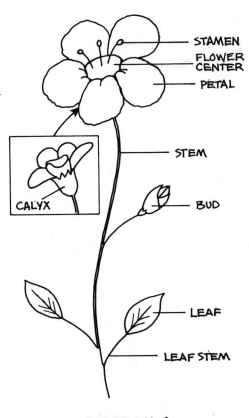

STAMEN
FLOWER CENTER
PETAL
STEM
CALYX
BUD
LEAF
LEAF STEM

DIAGRAM A

15

TINTING

Most of the time you'll be able to buy fabric in a color that suits your flowers, because most fabrics come in a vast array of colors. But occasionally you won't be able to find the exact color you want, and then you will want to apply the color to a white or off-white fabric by tinting. When deciding on your color or colors, let color pictures of flowers in books and seed catalogs be your guide.

And remember that if your flower requires sizing (i.e., stiffening the fabric), you'll have to tint it *before* the sizing can be applied.

Note: If the desired color is a solid, you can simply add the tint to the sizing mixture. (See Sizing, opposite.)

FOR SOLID-COLOR PETALS

To begin tinting, mix a commercial liquid dye with boiling water in a pint or quart jar, following directions on the package. Continue adding dye to the water until the desired color is achieved—test it on a paper towel or on a scrap of the fabric you're using for the flower.

When satisfied with the color, immerse the petal or petal unit in the dye, then remove it after a minute or two with a spoon, fork or kitchen tongs. Lay the petal on aluminum foil or wax paper until completely dry. (Do not use paper towels, grocery bags or the like, because the petal will stick and pick up lint.)

After applying the dye, if you decide the color is too intense, smooth out the petal while it is drying with a wet sponge to remove excess color.

FOR VARIEGATED PETALS

Tint these, using whichever of the following methods is most suitable for your flower. With all of these methods, you have to hang the petal upside down to dry in order to prevent the dye from running back into the center of the petal and ruining the effect.

(a) Tie-dye the upper part of the petal edges by wrapping the center of the petal with a piece of wire and holding the wrapped part out of the dye. (Diagram B.)

(b) Dip only the edges of the petal into the liquid dye.

(c) Tint the edges or the center of the petal by applying acrylic paint with a small artist's paintbrush. (Diagram C.)

(d) Paint stripes on the petal, using liquid dye applied with a small artist's paintbrush.

If you wish, you may use watercolor paints for these methods of tinting, applying it with a small artist's paintbrush that is fairly dry.

DIAGRAM B

SIZING

The purpose of sizing is to add stiffening to silks and gauzy fabrics so they'll hold their shape. If your fabric is not being tinted, the sizing is applied to it immediately after cutting out the patterns.

If you are tinting, wait until the dye or paint has dried completely before applying the sizing—and use only as much sizing as you need, because the dye is apt to bleed into the mixture.

As mentioned previously, for solid-color petals, you can save a step by simply adding your tint to the sizing formula and proceed as for sizing.

We have concocted a marvelous sizing formula after much trial and error, and you'll apply it to many flower-making fabrics when directed. Our sizing gives your flowers the soft texture and appearance reminiscent of real flowers, so no wonder we're proud of it.

SIZING FORMULA

Mix 2 ounces of white resin glue with 2 ounces of matte-finish Mod Podge, and add 6 ounces of water. (Do not under any circumstances use Mod Podge in

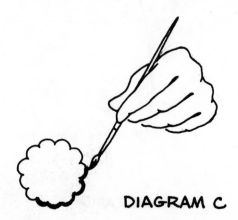

DIAGRAM C

regular finish, or your flowers will not look realistic.)

Stir the mixture thoroughly in a glass jar and store tightly capped. It will keep for a week or two. If you're adding a tint, you can do it either before storing or just before using.

Note that if you're working with especially light or heavy fabric, you may have to alter the proportions of the sizing ingredients slightly to get the correct sizing texture for the fabric.

APPLYING THE SIZING

When ready to apply the sizing, lay your petals or leaves on wax paper or aluminum foil. Dip a clean sponge brush or cosmetics sponge into the sizing and go over the petals with the sponge until they are completely saturated. Let the petals dry completely on the paper or foil, preferably overnight.

If you are making flowers in quantity, you may find it easier and faster to apply the sizing to a whole piece of fabric before cutting out the petals or leaves —if you do this, be sure to dry the fabric indoors on a clothesline or drying rack, with newspapers underneath to catch any drip.

SHAPING PETALS AND LEAVES

CUPPING

Cupping is a way of shaping a flower petal or leaf so that the edges fold slightly in or out, depending on the nature of the flower.

Cupping unwired petals and leaves: Lay the petal or leaf in the palm of your hand and press against it to make an indentation from top to bottom, as indicated by the dotted line in Diagram D. To make the indentation, you can use the tip of your fingernail, the tip of a knitting needle, a demitasse spoon or a burnisher (an inexpensive tool available at crafts stores). If the petal or leaf is made out of silk, do not attempt to cup it until after the sizing has been applied (page 16). If you find cupping difficult because the fabric is stiff

(and it usually is after sizing), hold the fabric over a steaming teakettle for a few seconds before you do the cupping.

Cupping wired petals and leaves: Lay the wired petal or leaf in the palm of your hand and press against it from the inside, gently shaping the hidden wire. Revolve a completed flower from wire to wire until you've shaped each petal in the flower.

CURLING

Curling is the technique used for shaping the tip and side edges of a petal and for wrinkling the petal to achieve a more natural look.

Curling an edge inward: Roll the petal over a ridged pencil toward you.

Curling an edge outward: Roll the petal away from you over the pencil. While the petal is tightly rolled over the pencil, you can also wrinkle the edge by squeezing the rolled petal from both sides toward the center, using your thumbs and index fingers.

Curling tiny petals: Curl them by using a knitting needle instead of a pencil.

FLUTING

Stretching a petal along the top edge to obtain a rippled or ruffled effect is known as fluting. Hold the edge of the petal with both thumbs and forefingers, keeping them about one-eighth inch apart, and gently tug the fabric back and forth, continuing along the edge until it is as rippled as desired.

FRINGING

To create a fringed effect on a flower, take découpage or manicure scissors and make little slashes along the edge of the petals, as shown in Diagram E.

DIAGRAM E

WIRING PETALS AND LEAVES

WHEN WIRE IS HIDDEN

Many petals and leaves have a characteristic shape that can only be achieved by wiring, especially if one is using silk or other flexible material. To hide the wiring, it is sandwiched between two layers of your petal or leaf (which is why you often cut 2

DIAGRAM D

17

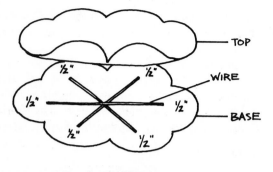

DIAGRAM F

pattern pieces for every part that needs wiring). You will use either #20 or #22 stem wire for this, as directed.

Wiring a petal unit: When working with these, cut to size half as many pieces of wire as there are petals in the unit. (Diagram F.) Cut each wire one inch shorter than the diameter of the petal unit.

Place one petal unit, wrong side up, on your work surface. Put some white resin glue on a piece of aluminum foil, and dip a toothpick into it. Using tweezers, pick up a wire and use the toothpick to apply glue to it along one side. Lay it sticky side down across the petal unit, leaving a half-inch margin at each end. Do the same with the other wires in turn, placing them as shown.

Apply more glue along the tops of the wires and place the second petal unit directly on top, wrong side down.

Protect with a piece of wax paper or aluminum foil on top, and press flat with a suitable weight until completely dry.

Wiring single petals and leaves: Follow the same procedure, but use only one long central wire, again positioning it so it comes to within half an inch of the tip. Cut enough wire to allow some excess to extend down—this will be used later, when attaching the petal or leaf to the main stem wire. (Diagram G.)

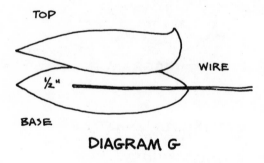

DIAGRAM G

WHEN WIRE IS NOT HIDDEN

Sometimes the petal or leaf wiring is done with covered wire in a matching color. In this case, the wire is glued to the wrong side, exactly as for hidden

wires. The wire remains visible, but the petal or leaf is usually turned so the wire doesn't show when the flower is assembled.

Sometimes the wire is covered with a small strip of matching fabric glued over its length. This is done when many petals are bunched together (as in the Cabbage Rose), so wiring is hidden.

HIGHLIGHTING

Highlighting means touching up a flower with additional color to give it a more realistic appearance. The tools that can be used for highlighting are a fine-tip crayon, a fine-tip oil pencil (we recommend Derwent pencils), a chalk sharpened to a fine point, or acrylic or watercolor paints applied with a small, almost-dry artist's paintbrush.

When highlighting is recommended, take one of these tools and apply the color *very delicately* to the petals of your flower, around the flower center, or elsewhere on the petals as directed for the individual flower. Usually highlighting is applied after the flower has been completely assembled, though if the assembly is extremely tight, with many petals quite close together, the individual petals should be highlighted before they are assembled.

Because highlighting is the technique that makes your flower equal to those expensive ones with their exquisite detail, it is important to use an extremely light touch—remember, a little highlighting goes a long way.

VEINING

When veins are desired on a leaf, as shown in Diagram H, they can be applied in several ways.

ON FABRIC

Veins are usually done with a sharp object such as a toothpick, knitting needle or tapestry needle. However, the veins can also be made with a fine-point felt-tip marking pen in a darker shade of green than the leaf.

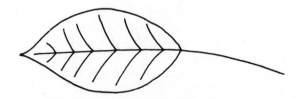

DIAGRAM H

ON OTHER MATERIALS

For leaves made of aluminum or some other equally hard material, make vein lines by indenting with an ice pick or awl or empty ball-point pen. Press just enough to make an impression; be careful not to cut through.

PRESSING FLAT

When you are directed to press flat a petal or a leaf, put a piece of wax paper or aluminum foil over it for protection. Then weight it down with heavy books or other suitable weight. The same procedure can be applied to flattening pieces of aluminum can.

DRYING

A block of styrofoam measuring about 12 x 15 x 2 inches can be extremely handy when it comes to drying a flower that has been painted, glued or varnished. If it has already been wired, all you have to do is stick the flower upright into the styrofoam until it is completely dry. This is also a convenient way to highlight a flower without having to hold it.

TAPING THE STEM WIRE

Taping is what you do to cover bare stem wire. For this, you almost always use floral tape, though occasionally you'll use silk or cotton floss or ribbon. Floral tape comes in several shades of green and brown—choose the shade most suitable for the flower you are making. Note that floral tape is stretchy, and it will adhere to itself if you tape as directed.

TAPING WITH FLORAL TAPE

Starting and finishing: Begin taping a stem wire at the top, directly below the flower petals or leaves. Leave a 1-inch tail of tape free, as shown in Diagram I. Proceed to tape down on a slant, in spiral fashion, wrapping over the 1-inch tail at the top, and slightly overlapping each row of tape. Be sure to slightly pull or stretch the tape as you wrap, because this makes it adhere to the wire. Cut off the tape at the end and press the stem so it adheres.

Breaking off: To stop taping in the middle, just cut off the tape and press it to the stem so it adheres. To continue again in the same place, just press on a new piece and start taping down again.

Note that you only wrap an excess or "tail" of tape at the top of a stem, just beneath the flower, to give the characteristic slight bulging shape there.

For tiny or tight areas: In these cases, always cut the tape in half lengthwise before starting to tape.

TAPING WITH FLOSS OR RIBBON

Floss and ribbon should be secured to the stem wire with a drop of glue before starting to tape. Wind closely in spiral fashion. For ribbon, slightly overlap each row as you go. Cut off at the bottom and secure with a drop of glue. (Hold with a paper clip until dry.)

LENGTHENING STEMS

You can lengthen a flower stem by taping another piece of stem wire to the original wire with floral tape. Let the wires overlap several inches on large flowers and an inch or so on smaller ones. Just hold the wires together as you tape (do not twist them). The tape will bind them together. (Diagram J.) This is especially helpful in flower arranging.

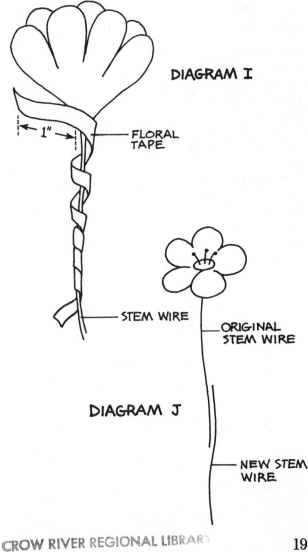

DIAGRAM I

1"

FLORAL TAPE

STEM WIRE

DIAGRAM J

ORIGINAL STEM WIRE

NEW STEM WIRE

ATTACHING LEAVES OR GRASSES
TO THE STEM WIRE

LEAVES

Start taping down the main stem as usual. When it's time to attach a leaf, hold the bottom of the leaf stem (or the bottom of the leaf, as directed) in position against the main stem. Just continue taping down, binding in the leaf stem as you tape.

GRASSES

Attach grasses in the same way, taping in an inch or so of the bottom of the grass to secure.

ATTACHING STAMENS TO THE STEM WIRE

BY TAPING

This is usually done with single stamens (those with a head at one end). Hold stamen (or cluster) and stem wire together so they overlap. Take a piece of floral tape and start taping down, binding them together, following directions for Taping the Stem Wire.

BY WIRING

Overlapping: Hold stamen (or cluster) and stem wire so they overlap, and wrap around with a bit of spool wire to secure. (Diagram K.) Cut off wire very close, unless directed otherwise. The wrapping wire is concealed by tape, as directed.

Hooking: This is done with double stamens (those with a head at each end). Fold stamen (or cluster) in half. Make a small hook at the top of the stem wire

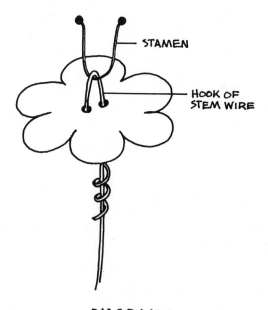

DIAGRAM L

and hook over the folded stamen. The hook is twisted around the stem to secure (Diagram L) and concealed by tape, as directed. Depending on the individual flower, petal units may be attached before the hook is secured.

BY WIRING AND TAPING

Usually done with delicate double stamens. The stamens are folded in half and bound together at the fold with fine spool wire. The bound stamens and stem wire are overlapped and taped together.

ATTACHING FABRIC OR RIBBON BOWS

Small bows may be made by pressing a piece of fabric together in the center, butterfly fashion, and winding around with spool wire to secure. Allow a few inches of extra wire at the end to attach to your flowers. (Diagram M.) This is good for tulle or other stiffened sheer fabric.

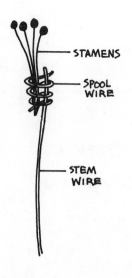

DIAGRAM K

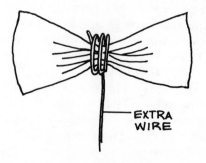

DIAGRAM M

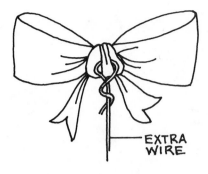

DIAGRAM N

Or you can make a proper bow, then loop spool wire through the back of the knot. Allow a few extra inches of wire at the end to attach to your flowers. (Diagram N.)

BEADING

There's nothing easier than making our beaded flowers and leaves. In principle, you string your beads onto fine spool wire, wrap the wire around and around in concentric rows to form a flat petal or leaf—then you lace the rows invisibly together with fine wire to hold their shape. Calyxes, flower centers and buds are made of loops of beads twisted together.

THE BEADS

For our flowers we use only one size of bead—size 11^0—and they're sold in bunches in many colors at your local crafts store. Each bunch contains about a dozen 20-inch strands—more than enough for any of our flowers.

THE WIRE

For the beading you'll use #28 spool wire; use #28 green spool wire for beading leaves. For the lacing, #32 lacing wire, also on a spool. We use them in silver or gold, and you'll find them at your crafts store.

TOOLS

Most of these you'll have around the house: a ruler (for measuring the rows of beads); an old pair of scissors or nail clippers (for cutting spool wire); wire cutters (for cutting clumps of wire); a pair of pliers. Note that even fine wire will mar the cutting edge of your scissors—so it's best to keep them for wire-cutting alone.

MAKING A BEADED PETAL OR LEAF

Transferring the beads to spool wire: Unwind about 2 feet of #28 spool wire, but do not cut the wire from the spool. With the right hand holding the wire and the left hand holding a strand of 11^0 beads, transfer all the beads onto the wire. (Diagram O.) (Left-handers will reverse these directions.) Crimp the end of the wire so the beads won't slip off. (Diagram P.)

The basic row: This is the start of the work, and its length determines the size of the finished piece.

1. If the basic row is to be 1 inch, say, this means that you measure off 1 inch of beads and push them up the spool wire to about 3 inches from the crimped end. (Diagram P.)

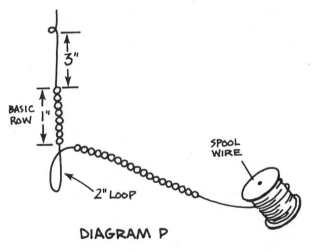

DIAGRAM P

2. Make a 2-inch loop of empty spool wire below these beads and twist it to secure. (Diagram O.)

To make a rounded petal or leaf:

1. Always starting at the loop end of the basic row, pull up some more beads and press them up close along the left side to the top of the basic row. Now with bared wire, go straight across the front of the wire atop the basic row. Give it a tight twist

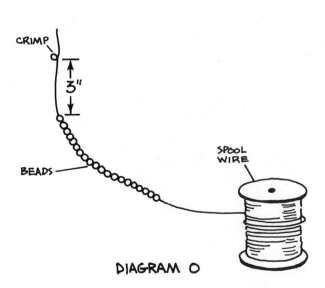

DIAGRAM O

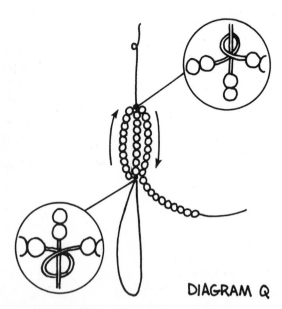

DIAGRAM Q

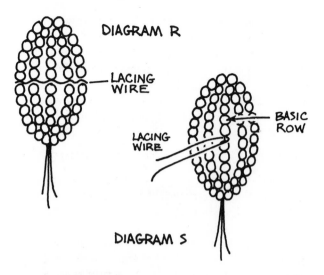

DIAGRAM R

DIAGRAM S

around, maintaining a 90° angle, as shown in Diagram Q.

2. Pull up some more beads and continue down the right side of the basic row in the same way—this time bringing the bared wire straight across the front of the wire below the basic row. Give it a tight twist around, again maintaining a 90° angle. (Diagram Q.)

3. Repeat Steps 1 and 2 for as many rows as directed. Just remember that every time you cross the basic row, top or bottom, you cross *in front* of it, twisting around once before continuing.

4. At the end of your last row, give your bared spool wire 2 or 3 tight twists, together with the loop wire at the bottom. (Hold the bead rows flat with one hand while twisting the wires with the other.)

5. To finish off the bottom: Cut off the spool wire to the same length as the loop. Cut the loop open at the bottom—you now have a clump of 3 wires serving as a stem.

6. To finish off the top: Cut off the crimped end of the wire ¼ inch above the top bead. Press wire back to the underside.

To make a pointed petal or leaf:

1. Starting at the loop end of the basic row, pull up more beads and press them up close along the left side to the top of the basic row. This time add 1 or 2 extra beads at the top. Then with bared wire, go across the front of the wire atop the basic row. Give it a tight twist around, this time maintaining a 45° angle.

2. Pull up some more beads, symmetrically adding 1 or 2 extra at the top. Then continue down the right side to the bottom of the basic row. Bring the bared wire across and twist it as in Step 2 for a rounded petal or leaf.

3. Repeat Steps 1 and 2 for as many rows as directed.

4. To finish off, follow Steps 4, 5 and 6 for a rounded petal or leaf.

Note that when a petal or leaf has a pointed top and a rounded bottom, you follow the appropriate directions for each end.

LACING

This secures your flat beading rows to each other so they hold their shape. Our lacing is done with very fine wire (as thin as thread), concealed between the beads. In essence, what you are doing is backstitching across the wrong side of the petal or leaf with the lacing wire, as shown in Diagram R.

1. Cut a maximum of 12 to 18 inches of #32 lacing wire.

2. Fold it exactly in half and insert both ends into the beading, so they straddle the wire of the basic row between 2 beads. (Diagram S.)

3. Turn to the other side and twist the 2 ends of lacing wire close to the beading.

4. Take 1 strand of the lacing wire and work out to the right, bringing it around the wire of the row next to the basic row. (Diagram T.)

BASIC ROW

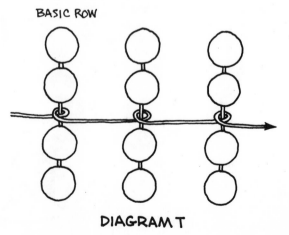

DIAGRAM T

5. Repeat Step 4, securing every row till you come to the last.

6. To finish off, twist the lacing wire twice around the outside row. Cut off the lacing wire on the wrong side, very close to the beading.

7. Pick up the remaining strand of lacing wire and repeat Steps 4 to 6, working out to the left of the basic row.

LOOPED CALYXES, FLOWERS AND BUDS

Here you're forming continuous loops and later fastening them together in a circle or clump.

1. Transfer your beads to the spool wire, as directed on page 21.

2. Push some beads up to about 3 inches of the crimped end of the wire. Measure off the length of beads called for—1 inch, say. Now twist your inch of beads into a loop, twisting tightly a few times to secure. (Hold the loop flat with one hand while twisting with the other.)

3. Repeat Step 2 for as many loops as directed. Try to keep them fairly close together, as shown in Diagram U.

DIAGRAM U

SOME WORKING TIPS

Along with these basic techniques, we would like to share a few of our trade secrets to speed you on your way to creating perfect flowers—every time. Here are some of the things we do to achieve great results:

- When you are ready to start, have all the required materials laid out so you won't have to scurry around looking for some tool or supply and interrupt the flow of creativity.
- If you are making more than one flower, use the assembly line approach by doing all the tracing at one time, cutting at one time, gluing at one time and so on.
- Once you have drawn a pattern on tracing paper and used it, transfer the pattern from the paper to a piece of cardboard and save in a marked envelope for the next time you need it. Or cut several patterns from the tracing paper and save these in the envelope.
- Keep on hand plenty of floral tape and #28 covered wire, because they are used in so many projects. The covered wire is sold on spools or in hanks, though it can also be purchased by the yard.
- When cutting stem wire, always use wire cutters or a pair of pliers instead of scissors to prevent ruining a good pair of the latter.
- Painting, gluing, varnishing and other such activities should be done in a well-ventilated area, but not outdoors, unless the space is protected. Take weather into account: A sticky day will produce a sticky finish, which is why an air-conditioned room is the ideal place to work if the temperature is above 80°.
- Always let glue, paint and sealer dry *completely* after application before you move on to the next step.
- Always apply glue sparingly so no part of the flower is damaged. A toothpick makes the best applicator.

PART II

CREATING THE FLOWERS

Some Flowers Made from Silk and Cotton

Bachelor's button, page 30

Black-eyed Susan, page 32

Anemone, page 27

Daffodil, page 38

Evening corsage, page 35

Flower from bridal bouquet, page 33

Detail from corsage, page 35

THREE:

Flowers from Silk and Cotton

Fabric flowers can run the gamut from small to large, casual to elegant, period to modern, simple to elaborate. They can be created from such diverse materials as silk, velvet, burlap and lace, to name but a few. The flowers we present here are the same ones that cost a fortune in boutiques and department stores, which is why we think they're pretty sensational. Even a few will provide the finishing touch to a room by emphasizing its period, color scheme or style.

Almost any fabric is suitable except heavy upholstery fabric, stretchy knits and some synthetics. For silk flowers, which originated in eighteenth-century France, we recommend using silk-like substitutes because real silk is often difficult to find. However, if you can find pure silk in white, remember you can

dye it any shade you wish. The exquisite Rambler Roses on page 66 are made of pure silk; needless to say, to buy them ready-made would be beyond most budgets.

Unless you happen to have scraps of material in the colors you want, you'll often have to buy one-fourth yard of material, even if you only need a small piece for your flower. However, you'll have enough left over to make quite a few more flowers, or to add to your scrap basket for the future.

As we mentioned earlier, always cut petals on the bias of the fabric to avoid raveling. If the fabric ravels anyway, go over the edges of the petals very lightly with white resin glue, using a toothpick as an applicator.

Anemone

One of the most graceful of spring flowers, the anemone looks best in a bouquet of assorted colors. It consists of 2 petal units (tinted, sized and wired) and a flower center (a tiny cotton ball covered with a bit of fabric). Assemble your petals and storebought stamens around the center, attach the stem wire, and finish by taping, adding a storebought calyx and 3 leaves.

MATERIALS FOR 1 FLOWER AND 3 LEAVES

PETAL UNITS

¼ yard silk lining in white or celadon
commercial liquid dye (or watercolor paint) in desired color
sizing formula (page 16)
6 pieces #20 stem wire, each 4½ inches long
white resin glue

FLOWER CENTER

3-inch square of black silk fabric (or scrap of nylon hose and black commercial dye)
absorbent cotton cosmetics ball
#32 spool wire

FLOWER ASSEMBLY AND STEM

8-inch piece #16 stem wire
20 black single craft stamens
green floral tape
craft calyx
3 medium-size craft leaves (chrysanthemum type)

HIGHLIGHTING (OPTIONAL)

felt-tip marking pen (or acrylic paint) in color to match flower

Also: pencil, ruler, tissue paper, scissors; wire cutters; sponge brush or cosmetics sponge (to apply sizing); tweezers, toothpicks, wax paper or aluminum foil (for gluing); small paintbrush (for watercolor or acrylic paint) if highlighting

PETAL UNITS

1. Make your tissue paper pattern for petal unit, tracing from book Pattern 1.

2. Cut out 4 petal units (to make 2 finished petals). Fold the silk fabric, right sides facing. Place pattern as shown in Diagram A, pin, and cut out twice.

3. Tint the petal units by tie-dyeing with liquid dye or painting with watercolor. Anemone petals are deep-colored at edges and whitish at the base, so you tint only the edges.

4. Apply sizing to the tinted petal units. Set aside to dry.

5. Using 3 pieces of the #20 stem wire, wire 2 petal units, making 1 finished petal unit. Repeat with the remaining 2 petal units, to make 2 finished units.

FLOWER CENTER

1. Use a 3-inch-square scrap of black silk (or dye a scrap of nylon hose with commercial liquid dye, following package directions. Let dry thoroughly.)

2. Divide the absorbent cotton cosmetics ball into 2 small balls. Cover 1 ball smoothly with the black silk, drawing the fabric together underneath. (Diagram B.) Secure it around tightly with a bit of #32 spool wire, but do not cut the wire off the spool. Trim off excess fabric, leaving ¼ inch below wire. (Save the other cotton ball for another flower.)

PATTERN 1

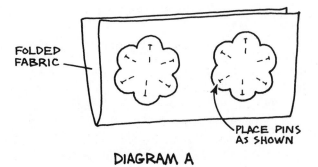

DIAGRAM A

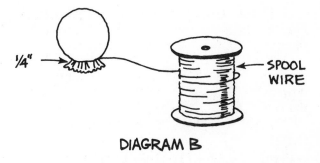

DIAGRAM B

FLOWER ASSEMBLY AND STEM

1. Push one end of the stem wire ½ inch up into the bottom of the flower center.

2. Secure the stamens around the flower center, continuing with the spool wire, wrapping it around tightly as in Diagram C, then cut off the spool wire very close.

3. Now, using the floral tape, start taping the stem wire. Start at the top and tape 1½ inches down. Cut off the tape.

4. With the tip of your scissors, make a tiny hole in the exact center of each wired petal unit. Put the stem wire down through the holes and push the petal units up the stem until both are snug against the flower center. Make sure petal units are turned so petal tips are staggered.

5. Push the calyx up the stem wire right under the petal units.

6. Start again with the floral tape and continue taping down the stem for another 2 inches.

7. Attach the first leaf to the stem. Continue taping another 1½ inches down the stem.

8. Attach the second leaf to the stem opposite the first leaf. Continue taping another 1½ inches down the stem.

9. Attach the third leaf on the same side as the first. Finish taping down to the bottom of the stem. Cut off tape.

10. Shape the flower by cupping petal units to anemone shape and curling the individual petal edges.

HIGHLIGHTING (OPTIONAL)

If you like, highlight the flower petals with a felt-tip marking pen (or a fine brush and acrylic paint).

THE CREATIVE TOUCH

Our anemones are combined with a fern plant and displayed in a hollowed-out tree trunk which can be purchased at a crafts store or garden center. Or try arranging a bouquet in assorted colors in a silver chafing dish with cut fern kept damp in Oasis.

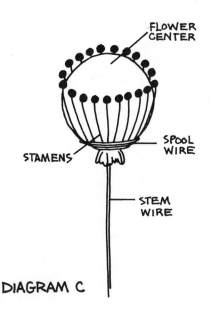

DIAGRAM C

Bachelor's Button

This charming blue flower is very simple to make. It consists of 3 petal units (with pinked edges, sized and highlighted). Storebought stamens and a calyx are attached with the stem wire and finished by taping, adding 2 storebought leaves.

MATERIALS FOR 1 FLOWER AND 2 LEAVES

PETAL UNITS

3 x 8-inch piece silk lining in royal blue
sizing formula (page 16)
white watercolor or acrylic paint

FLOWER ASSEMBLY AND STEM

5 white double craft stamens
8-inch piece #20 stem wire
craft calyx (carnation type)
green floral tape
2 small craft leaves (chrysanthemum type)

Also: compass, pencil, tissue paper, scissors, pinking shears; wire cutters; sponge brush or cosmetics sponge (to apply sizing); wax paper or aluminum foil; small paintbrush (for watercolor or acrylic paint)

PETAL UNITS

1. With a compass draw 3 circles on tissue paper, each measuring 2¼ inches in diameter. Cut them out. These are your petal unit patterns.

2. Place patterns on silk fabric, pin, and cut around them with pinking shears to make your petal units. (Diagram A.)

3. Fold each petal unit in half, then in quarters, then in eighths. Trim the tops with pinking shears, if necessary. While petals are still folded, cut off the top corners with regular scissors. (Diagram B.)

4. Unfold petal units and apply sizing. Put aside to dry.

5. Highlight each petal with white paint.

DIAGRAM B

FLOWER ASSEMBLY AND STEM

1. Fold stamens in half. Make a small hook at one end of the #20 stem wire and hook this over the folded stamens. (Diagram C.)

FOLDED STAMENS

DIAGRAM C

STEM WIRE

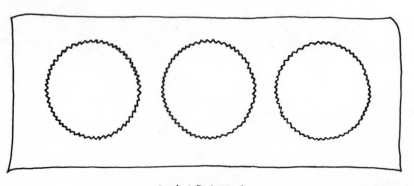

DIAGRAM A

2. With the tip of your scissors, cut 2 tiny holes in the exact center of each petal unit. Attach the petal units by pushing the bottom of the stem wire and the hook end down through the 2 holes in all 3 petal units. Press the hook and stem wire close together underneath.

3. Push the calyx up the stem wire close under the flower (catching in the hook as well), then twist the hook around the stem wire to secure. (Diagram D.)

4. Start at the top with the floral tape and tape ½ inch down the stem wire.

5. Attach the first leaf to the stem. Continue taping another 1½ inches down the stem.

6. Attach the second leaf to the stem opposite the first leaf. Continue taping down to the bottom of the stem. Cut off tape.

7. Fan out the petals for a fluffy effect and flute the edges.

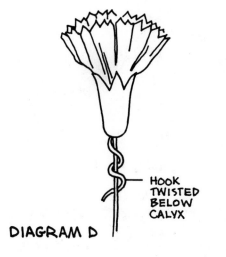

HOOK
TWISTED
BELOW
CALYX

DIAGRAM D

BACHELOR'S BUTTON BUD (OPTIONAL)

You can make a bud by omitting the stamens and the calyx and wrapping around the base of the folded petals with floral tape. Insert the stem wire before wrapping and continue taping to the bottom of the stem wire. Or, the bud can be attached to the main stem of a flower.

THE CREATIVE TOUCH

Combine a few bachelor's buttons with some statice and arrange in a pewter tankard for a man's desk.

Black-Eyed Susan

Very easy. It consists of a gathered felt petal unit and a pompon flower center. The center is taped to the stem wire and inserted into the petal unit. It is finished by taping, adding in 2 (wired) felt leaves.

MATERIALS FOR 1 FLOWER AND 2 LEAVES

PETAL UNIT

1 x 4-inch piece yellow felt
thread to match yellow felt

FLOWER CENTER

black craft pompon (or small ball fringe)

LEAVES

8-inch-square piece green felt
2 pieces #20 stem wire, each 3 inches long
white resin glue

FLOWER ASSEMBLY AND STEM

8-inch piece #18 stem wire
tacky glue
green floral tape

Also: pencil, tissue paper, scissors; sewing needle; wire cutters; tweezers, toothpicks, wax paper or aluminum foil (for gluing)

PETAL UNIT

1. Make a tissue paper pattern, tracing from book Pattern 1. Cut 1 petal unit from the yellow felt from Pattern 1, taking care not to slash closer than ¼ inch from the top.
2. With needle and yellow thread, sew a running stitch across the straight edge of the petal unit, as shown in Diagram A. Pull the thread tightly, gather-

ing the petal unit so petals fan out to form a flower. Tack the first and last petals together, knotting the thread to secure. (Diagram B.)

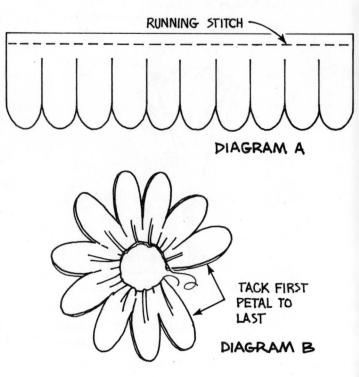

DIAGRAM A

TACK FIRST PETAL TO LAST

DIAGRAM B

LEAVES

1. Make a tissue paper pattern, tracing from book Pattern 2.
2. Cut 4 leaves (to make 2 finished leaves) out of green felt from Pattern 2.
3. Using 1 piece of the #20 stem wire and glue, wire 2 leaves together, making 1 finished leaf. Repeat with the remaining 2 leaves, to make 2 finished leaves.

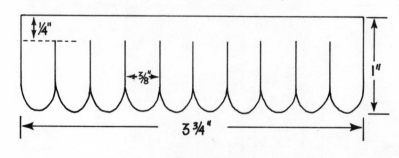

PATTERN 1

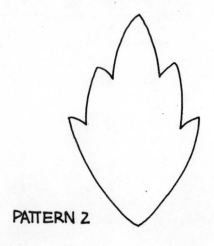

PATTERN 2

FLOWER ASSEMBLY AND STEM

1. Dip one end of the stem wire into glue and push up into the bottom of the pompon (or ball fringe). Attach with floral tape. Cut off tape.

2. Insert stem wire down into the middle of the gathered petal unit until flower center rests snugly against the petals. Start again with the tape just below the flower center and tape down the stem for 2 inches.

3. Attach the first leaf to the stem. Continue taping down another inch.

4. Attach the second leaf to the stem opposite the first leaf and finish taping down to the bottom of the stem. Cut off tape.

THE CREATIVE TOUCH

A bird's nest makes a novel container for the black-eyed Susan. Buy the nest at your local crafts store and be sure to tuck in an artificial bird for good measure.

Bridal Bouquet

For all its opulent effect, this, too, is very simple to make. It consists of 3 large and 12 small rosebuds. Each is made by rolling numerous (sized) petals around a wire to form a tight ball. A stem wire is attached, and the bud is finished by taping, adding a storebought calyx. The rosebuds are inserted into a nosegay holder along with velvet craft leaves and decorated with satin streamers and tulle bows.

MATERIALS
FOR 15 ROSEBUDS AND 30 LEAVES

PETALS

1 yard bride's dress fabric
sizing formula (page 16)

FLOWER ASSEMBLY AND STEM

15 pieces green #28 covered wire, each 6 inches long
15 pieces #22 stem wire, each 6 inches long
green floral tape
12 craft calyxes (small rose size)
3 craft calyxes (large rose size)

BOUQUET ASSEMBLY

3 yards ½-inch double-faced satin ribbon in matching
    or complementary color
nosegay holder
Oasis
#28 spool wire
⅛ yard tulle in matching or complementary color
30 velvet craft leaves (in various rose sizes)

Also: pencil, tissue paper, scissors; wire cutters; sponge brush or cosmetics sponge (to apply sizing); wax paper or aluminum foil

PETALS

1. Make tissue paper patterns, tracing from book patterns. Cut 21 large petals out of fabric from Petal Pattern 1, and cut out 84 small petals following Petal Pattern 2.

2. Apply sizing to the petals. Set aside to dry.

PATTERN 1   PATTERN 2

DIAGRAM A

FLOWER ASSEMBLY AND STEM

1. Take 7 large petals, fold in half across the width, and slide them onto 1 piece of the green #28 covered wire, as shown in Diagram A.

2. Gather the petals together to one side of the wire (Diagram B). Then, starting at this end, roll up the petals and the wire tightly to form a large rosebud. (Diagrams C, D.)

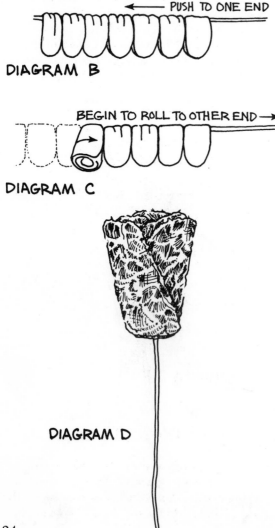

← PUSH TO ONE END

DIAGRAM B

BEGIN TO ROLL TO OTHER END →

DIAGRAM C

DIAGRAM D

3. Shape the outer petals by cupping.

4. Push the end of a piece of #22 stem wire up into the bottom of the rosebud and attach with floral tape. Cut off tape.

5. Push a large calyx up the stem wire right under the bud. Start again with the floral tape and tape down the stem wire to the end. Cut off tape.

6. Repeat Steps 1 to 5 to make 2 more large rosebuds.

7. Repeat steps 1 to 5, using the small calyxes, to make 12 small rosebuds (Petal Pattern 2).

BOUQUET ASSEMBLY

1. Cut the ribbon into 6 pieces, each half a yard long. Tie one end of each piece around the rim of the nosegay holder to form streamers.

2. Fit some Oasis into the holder, securing it with #28 spool wire.

3. Cut the piece of tulle into 6 pieces, each measuring 3 x 6 inches. Pinch each piece in the middle and wrap around tightly with #28 spool wire to form a bow. Cut off the spool wire, leaving a 6-inch tail to insert into the Oasis.

4. Insert the rosebuds, leaves and tulle bows into the nosegay holder in a random pattern.

THE CREATIVE TOUCH

This exquisite bouquet adds a lovely accent note to any wedding, as well as being a lasting treasure in years to come. Order extra fabric from the manufacturer of the bridal dress or purchase the extra fabric, if the dress is to be sewn at home—the same holds true for bouquets for bridesmaids as well. Only last June we were happy to make a friend's bridal bouquet out of white cotton eyelet—and for another wedding we helped the bridesmaids make their bouquets from a pale yellow organza print to match their dresses.

Evening Corsage

The five glittery flowers are made of 2 petal units (velvet, and organza sprinkled with Diamond Dust). Petals are assembled around a stamen taped to a stem wire, then all are attached to a main stem and wound with ribbon, adding a bow.

MATERIALS FOR CORSAGE
(5 FLOWERS AND 5 LEAVES)

PETAL UNITS

⅛ yard crushed velvet in desired color
⅛ yard matching silk organza
spray adhesive
Diamond Dust

FLOWER ASSEMBLY AND STEM

5 single craft stamens in desired color
5 pieces #22 stem wire, each 6 inches long
green floral tape

BOUQUET ASSEMBLY

5 small craft leaves (geranium or rose type)
6-inch piece #20 stem wire
1 yard corsage ribbon in desired color
#28 spool wire

Also: pencil, tissue paper, scissors; wire cutters; glue; wax paper or aluminum foil (for spraying)

PETAL UNITS

1. Make tissue paper pattern, tracing from book pattern. Use the pattern to cut 5 petal units out of velvet and 5 petal units out of organza.
2. Shape petals by curling the tips and edges.
3. Lightly mist organza petal units with spray adhesive. Let dry until tacky, then sprinkle lightly with Diamond Dust. Put aside until dry.

PATTERN 1

FLOWER ASSEMBLY AND STEM

1. Attach a stamen to one end of a piece of #22 stem wire, using floral tape. Cut off tape.
2. With the tip of your scissors, make a tiny hole in the exact centers of 1 velvet and 1 organza petal unit. Push the bottom of the stem wire down through the hole of the organza petal unit, then through the hole in the velvet unit, drawing it down until the bottom of the stamen is just below the petal units.
3. Make sure the 2 petal units are turned so petal tips are staggered, then start again with the floral tape and tape from the bottom of the flower down the stem wire to the end. Cut off tape.
4. Repeat Steps 1 to 3 to make 4 more flowers.

BOUQUET ASSEMBLY

1. Using floral tape, attach your 5 flowers and the 5 leaves to the #20 stem wire, placing them as shown in Diagram A.
2. Cover the stem wire by winding with the corsage ribbon, securing at the ends with a drop of glue.
3. Make a bow of the corsage ribbon, and use #28 spool wire to attach it among the flowers.

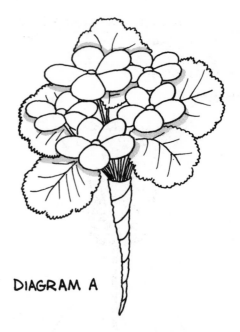

DIAGRAM A

THE CREATIVE TOUCH

Rejuvenate an old evening bag by covering it with cotton velveteen, gluing on a generous amount of rhinestone trim, and wiring this corsage to the handle or pinning it to the top with a corsage pin.

Cyclamen Plant

Here is a whole cyclamen plant to place in a pot. Flowers are made of petal units (sized and highlighted) taped to a stem (including a craft pep in the center). The flower base is built up with floral tape, and petals are glued back to hold their shape. Bud petals are wrapped around with a green fabric calyx, then taped to the stem wire. To finish, flowers, buds and craft leaves are lashed together and taped.

MATERIALS FOR 1 PLANT
(6 FLOWERS, 2 BUDS AND 5 LEAVES)

FLOWER PETAL UNITS AND BUD PETALS

¼ yard moiré in desired color
sizing formula (page 16)
fine felt-tip marking pen in shade deeper than moiré
 (optional)

FLOWER ASSEMBLY AND STEM

2 yards #20 stem wire
6 white single craft peps
green floral tape
tacky glue

BUD ASSEMBLY AND STEM

small piece green cotton fabric
#32 spool wire

PLANT ASSEMBLY

5 large craft leaves (African violet type)

Also: pencil, tissue paper, scissors; sponge brush or cosmetics sponge (to apply sizing); wax paper or aluminum foil; wire cutters

FLOWER PETAL UNITS AND BUD PETALS

1. Make tissue paper Patterns 1 and 2, tracing from book patterns. Cut 6 flower petal units out of moiré from Pattern 1, and cut 4 bud petals out of moiré from Pattern 2.
2. Apply sizing to flower petal units and to bud petals; set aside to dry.
3. When dry, highlight flower petal units with the felt-tip pen (optional).

FLOWER ASSEMBLY AND STEM

1. Cut the #20 stem wire into 8 pieces, varying in length from 6 to 10 inches. Take 6 pieces for your flowers. (Set aside 2 pieces for the buds.)
2. With the tip of your scissors, make a tiny hole in the exact center of one of the petal units. Put 1 pep through the hole.
3. Place a piece of the #20 stem wire against the pep underneath the petal unit and join them with floral tape.

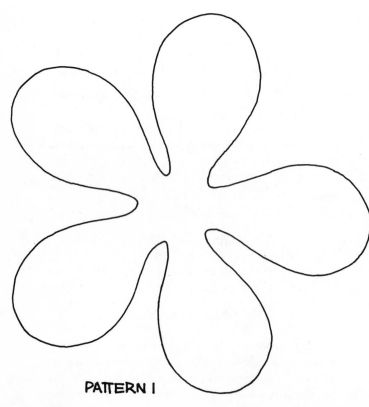

PATTERN 1

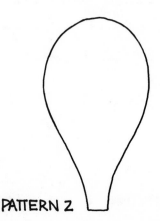

PATTERN 2

4. With the floral tape, build up the stem directly under the petal unit, as shown in Diagram A, then tape down the stem to the end. Cut off tape.

5. Apply glue liberally to the built-up area of the stem. While the glue is still wet, push back the petal unit with your fingers and pinch it into the glue. Hold in place until the glue sets.

6. Repeat Steps 1 to 5 to make 5 more cyclamen flowers.

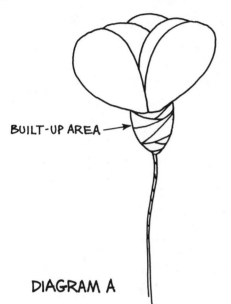

BUILT-UP AREA

DIAGRAM A

BUD ASSEMBLY AND STEM

1. Make tissue paper Pattern 3, tracing from book pattern. Cut 2 calyxes out of green cotton fabric from Pattern 3.

2. Take 2 of the bud petals and use #32 spool wire to wrap them together at their narrow ends.

3. Take one of the green fabric calyxes and wrap it around the wrapped bud petals to form a cone, gluing to secure. (Diagram B.)

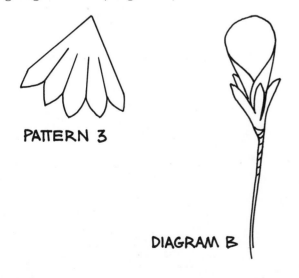

PATTERN 3

DIAGRAM B

4. Push the end of a piece of the #20 stem wire up into the bottom of the bud and attach with floral tape. Continue taping down to the bottom of the stem. Cut off tape.

5. Repeat Steps 1 to 4 for the second bud.

PLANT ASSEMBLY

1. Take 2 finished stems and use #32 spool wire to lash them together down the bottom 2 inches of their stems. Lash on the other stems, one at a time, in the same manner. (Diagram C.)

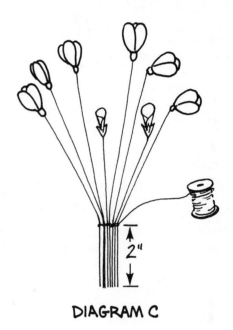

2"

DIAGRAM C

2. When finished with the stems, lash the leaf stems to the same place.

3. Tape over the lashed portion of wires with floral tape and insert your cyclamen plant in real soil in a clay pot. Or you can push it into a decorative planter filled with styrofoam and covered with dried moss.

THE CREATIVE TOUCH

This doesn't need anything beyond a pretty pot. We "planted" our cyclamen in an antique cachepot, but it would look equally attractive in a clay flowerpot as suggested above.

Daffodil

This lifelike spring flower is made of 2 petal units and a flower center (all sized). It is assembled by rolling the center around a storebought stamen attached to the stem wire and placing the petal units around the center. The stem is finished by taping, adding 2 (wired) leaves and 1 rolled "new" leaf.

MATERIALS FOR 1 FLOWER AND 3 LEAVES

FLOWER PETAL UNITS AND FLOWER CENTERS

¼ yard pale-to-medium yellow silk lining
⅛ yard bright yellow silk lining
sizing formula (page 16)

LEAVES

¼ yard dark green oilcloth
small scrap pale green silk lining
2 pieces #20 stem wire, each 8 inches long
white resin glue
green felt-tip marking pen
green floral tape

FLOWER ASSEMBLY AND STEM

yellow single craft stamen
8-inch piece #16 stem wire
clear craft cement

Also: pencil, tissue paper, scissors, pinking shears; sponge brush or cosmetics sponge (to apply sizing); wire cutters; tweezers, toothpicks, wax paper or aluminum foil (for gluing)

FLOWER PETAL UNITS AND FLOWER CENTERS

1. Make tissue paper Patterns 1 and 2, tracing from book patterns. Cut 2 petal units out of pale yellow silk from Pattern 1. Cut flower center out of bright yellow silk from Pattern 2, using regular scissors to cut the straight sides and pinking shears to cut the curved side.
2. Apply sizing to petal units and flower center. Set aside to dry.

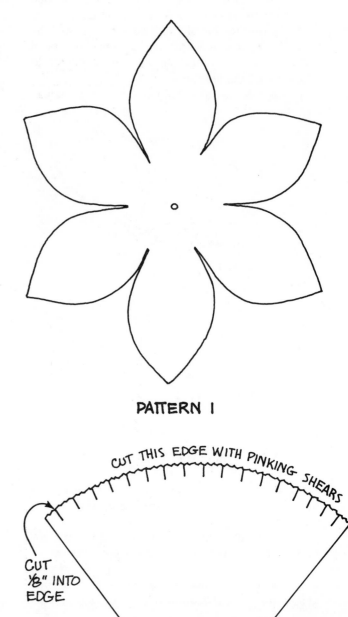

PATTERN 1

CUT THIS EDGE WITH PINKING SHEARS

CUT ⅛" INTO EDGE

PATTERN 2

PATTERN 3

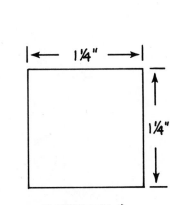

PATTERN 4

pale green silk from Pattern 4. Then roll the square piece of pale green silk to form a tight cone and secure it at the bottom with a small piece of floral tape. (Diagram A.)

DIAGRAM A

FLOWER ASSEMBLY AND STEM

1. Attach the stamen to one end of the #16 stem wire with floral tape.

2. Put a drop of clear craft cement at the bottom of the flower center and roll it tightly around the stamen to form a cone.

3. With the tip of your scissors, make a tiny hole in the exact centers of the 2 petal units. Put the stem wire down through the holes and push up both petal units until they are right under the flower center. Make sure the petal units are turned so petal tips are staggered.

4. Secure the bottom of the flower to the stem wire with floral tape, then tape down the stem wire for 2 inches.

5. Attach the new leaf to the stem with the tape. Continue taping another 4 inches down the stem.

6. Attach the 2 leaves to the stem—both at the same level, but opposite each other. Continue taping down to the end of the stem. Cut off tape.

7. Shape petals by cupping.

THE CREATIVE TOUCH

Arrange these springtime beauties in a white hat with some Pussy Willows (page 145) and Irises (page 48); or combine all three with a living plant as we did.

LEAVES

1. Make tissue paper Pattern 3, tracing from book pattern. Cut 4 leaves (to make 2 finished leaves) out of oilcloth from Pattern 3.

2. Take 2 of the leaves and, using glue, wire them together with 1 piece of the #20 stem wire. Mark veins of the wired leaf with the green felt-tip marking pen. Repeat with the remaining 2 leaves to make the second finished leaf.

3. For the "new" leaf, make tissue paper Pattern 4, tracing from the book pattern. Cut 1 new leaf out of

More Flowers from Silk and Cotton

Iris, page 48

Fuchsia stalk, page 44

Rubrum lily, page 50

Gingham flower, page 46

Poppy, page 52

Silk rose, page 55

Cabbage rose, page 58

Rose pin, page 63

Cabbage rose centerpiece, page 61

Shaggy zinnia, page 71

Desert Flower Sprig

Each of these tiny velvet flowers and its stamen is taped to a short stem wire. The sprig is assembled by taping the flower stems to the main stem—that's all there is to it.

MATERIALS FOR 1 SPRIG (7 FLOWERS)

PETAL UNITS

⅛ yard velvet, or ⅛ yard 1-inch velvet ribbon, in desired color
white resin glue

FLOWER ASSEMBLY AND STEM

7 yellow single craft stamens
7 pieces #22 stem wire, each 2 inches long
green floral tape

SPRIG ASSEMBLY

6-inch piece #20 stem wire

HIGHLIGHTING (OPTIONAL)

acrylic paint in desired color

Also: pencil, tissue paper, scissors; wire cutters; small paintbrush (for acrylic paint) if highlighting

PETAL UNITS

1. Coat the wrong side of the velvet lightly with the glue to prevent raveling. Set aside to dry.
2. Make tissue paper Petal Unit Pattern, tracing from book pattern. Cut 7 petal units out of velvet from pattern.

PATTERN 1

FLOWER ASSEMBLY AND STEM

1. With the tip of your scissors, make a tiny hole in the exact center of a petal unit and put a stamen into the hole.
2. Place the end of a piece of #22 stem wire against the stamen beneath the petal unit. Join them with floral tape, and continue taping down to the end of the stem. Cut off tape.
3. Repeat Steps 1 and 2 to make 6 more flowers.

SPRIG ASSEMBLY

Using floral tape, attach the stems of your 7 flowers to the #20 stem wire, placing them as shown in Diagram A. Then tape down the stem to the end. Cut off tape.

HIGHLIGHTING (OPTIONAL)

Highlight the flowers with acrylic paint (optional) in the center.

THE CREATIVE TOUCH

We like to see several sprigs of these desert flowers combined with cacti and succulents growing on an interesting formation of rock.

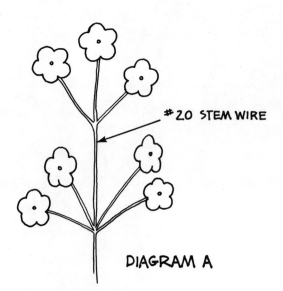

#20 STEM WIRE

DIAGRAM A

Oriental Fruit Blossom Branch

This charming composition is made of 20 variegated small double blossoms attached to a shapely tree branch set in a wooden base. Each blossom consists of 2 (sized) petal units drawn up around a cluster of craft stamens taped to a stem, and finished by taping. Note that you may buy pre-cut and shaped craft petal units for this, or make your own. Buy the branch from a crafts shop or florist, or use one from your own back yard.

MATERIALS FOR 1 FRUIT BLOSSOM BRANCH (20 BLOSSOMS, BRANCH AND BASE)

PETAL UNITS

40 pre-cut shaped craft petal units in desired colors
    (or 1/3 yard silk lining and sizing formula)

BLOSSOM ASSEMBLY AND STEM

20 clusters of single craft stamens (about 16 stamens
    per cluster)
20 pieces #22 stem wire, each 2½ inches long
brown floral tape

BRANCH AND BASE ASSEMBLY

tree branch (manzanita type)
7-inch-square découpage plaque or wooden block,
    ½ thick
white resin glue and/or nails

Also: pencil, tissue paper, scissors; sponge brush or cosmetics sponge (if cutting and sizing petal units); wire cutters, drill, hammer

PETAL UNITS

1. If pre-cut, trim petal units to the size of the Petal Unit Pattern. Or, make tissue paper pattern, tracing from book pattern. Cut 40 petal units out of silk lining from pattern.
2. Apply sizing to petal units. Set aside to dry.

BLOSSOM ASSEMBLY AND STEM

1. Cut each stamen cluster to ¾ inch.
2. Attach stamen cluster to the end of a piece of the #22 stem wire, using brown floral tape.
3. Take 2 petal units and, with the tip of your scissors, make a tiny hole in the exact center of each.
4. Put the stem wire down through the holes and push up both petal units until they are right under the stamen cluster. Make sure petal units are turned so petal tips are staggered.

5. Using floral tape, secure the petal units to the stem wire, then tape down the stem wire to the end. Cut off tape.
6. Repeat Steps 1 to 5 to make 19 more blossoms.

PATTERN I

BRANCH AND BASE ASSEMBLY

1. Drill a hole in the découpage plaque (or wooden block) to fit the diameter of your tree branch.
2. Secure the branch into the hole with glue. (You can also secure the branch by hammering a nail into the underside of the plaque.)
3. Using brown floral tape, tape the blossoms to the tree branch, allowing 1 inch of each stem to show. (See Diagram A for placement.)

THE CREATIVE TOUCH

Complete the composition by adding an Oriental figurine or two to dramatize the theme.

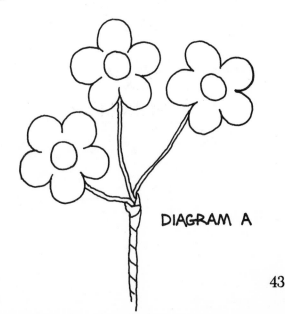

DIAGRAM A

43

Fuchsia Stalk

The lovely blossoms for this fuchsia stalk are made of white cotton (highlighted with pale pink watercolor) and deep pink silk (sized) petal units. For each flower, the finished petals are drawn up around a cluster of stamens attached to spool wire, the spool wire then taped to a white thread-stem. To finish, the 3 flowers, bud and 2 craft leaves are taped to a long stem wire-stalk.

MATERIALS FOR 3 FLOWERS, 1 BUD AND 2 LEAVES

PETAL UNITS

¼ yard white cotton
¼ yard fuchsia pink silk lining
sizing formula (page 16)
pale pink watercolor paint

FLOWER AND BUD ASSEMBLY

4 pieces #28 spool wire, each 2 inches long
9 white single craft stamens
green floral tape
white resin glue
4 pieces white heavy-duty thread, each 4½ inches long

STALK ASSEMBLY

2 craft leaves (rose type)
12-inch piece #16 stem wire
green floral tape

Also: pencil, tissue paper, scissors; sponge brush or cosmetics sponge (to apply sizing); wax paper or aluminum foil; small artist's paintbrush (for high-lighting); wire cutters

PATTERN I

PETAL UNITS

1. Make your tissue paper pattern, tracing from book Pattern 1. Cut 6 inner petal units out of white cotton from Pattern 1.
2. Make your tissue paper pattern, tracing from book Pattern 2. Cut 4 outer petal units from the silk lining, following Pattern 2. One of these will be used as a bud.

PATTERN 2

3. Apply sizing to the silk petal units. Set aside to dry.
4. With the small artist's paintbrush, highlight the inner area of the cotton petal units with pale pink watercolor paint, leaving the petal tips white. Set aside to dry.
5. Shape all petal units by curling the petal tips and edges.

FLOWER AND BUD ASSEMBLY

1. Attach 3 stamens to one end of a 2-inch piece of #28 spool wire with floral tape. Repeat twice, for a total of 3 pieces of spool wire with 3 stamens attached to each wire.
2. With the tip of your scissors, make a tiny hole in the exact center of each cotton petal unit. Take 2 of the cotton petal units and put the spool wire down through the holes. Push up both petal units until they are right under the stamens, making sure to stagger the placement of the petals.
3. Wrap 1 of the silk petal units around the cotton petals and secure with a tiny amount of glue where the edges meet.

4. Beginning directly under the petal units, build up ¼ inch down the spool wire with floral tape, as shown by the shaded area in Diagram A. Continue taping down the spool wire with the floral tape and

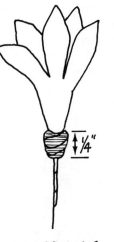

DIAGRAM A

attach one of the 4½-inch pieces of thread to it as shown in Diagram B. Tape to end of wire; cut off tape.

5. Repeat Steps 2 to 4 for 2 more flowers for a total of 3 finished flowers.

6. For a bud, wrap the remaining silk petal unit around the end of the remaining 2-inch piece of spool wire; secure the petal ends together with glue and attach the bud to the stem wire with floral tape.

7. Build up the stem wire at the base of the bud with floral tape. Continue taping down to the end of the spool wire, attaching the remaining 4¼-inch piece of thread as directed in Step 4 above.

STALK ASSEMBLY

1. Tape 1 of the craft leaves to the end of the #16 stem wire with floral tape, completely taping in all of the leaf's stem.

2. Continuing with the floral tape, tape 1 inch down the stem wire and attach 1 of the flowers by its white thread, letting about ¼ inch of the thread show between the flower and the stem wire. (Diagram C.)

3. Tape down the stem another inch and attach the bud in the same way you attached the flower.

4. Tape down the stem another inch or two and attach the second leaf to the stem opposite the first leaf.

5. Continue taping down the stem wire, attaching the remaining 2 flowers as you wish. Continue taping the stem to the end. Cut off tape.

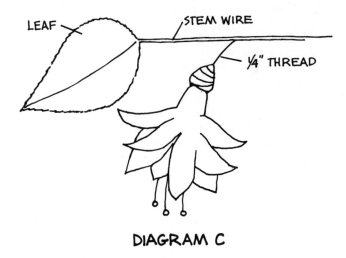

DIAGRAM C

THE CREATIVE TOUCH

Although it takes some time to make several stalks of fuchsia, the results are well worth the effort, as is proven by our old-fashioned birdcage filled with a mass of fuchsia and real plants; the fuchsia stems are inserted right into the soil of the plants.

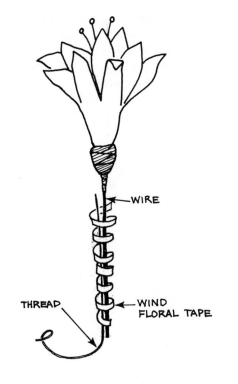

DIAGRAM B

Gingham Flower Stalk

Easiest of all: you bend pieces of covered wire to petal shape, glue them to your gingham, cut out closely around them—and there are your petals. Green ribbon leaves are made the same way. Petals are assembled around stamen clusters attached to stem wire. The small flower is attached to the top of the stalk, with the leaves and other flowers alternating below—all finished by taping.

Instead of using the patterns we give here, you can simply vary the size and shape of your petals and flowers as you wish—a petal-shaping tool from a crafts store will make this easy task even easier. To speed the work, bend and glue down all your petal and leaf wires and let them dry at the same time. After making the gingham flower stalk, try an entire bouquet of flowers using this simple procedure!

MATERIALS FOR 4 FLOWERS AND 5 LEAVES

FLOWER PETALS AND LEAVES

¼ yard gingham
½ yard green burlap ribbon, 1 inch wide
tacky glue
4 yards #28 covered wire in color compatible with
    gingham, cut as follows:
    for small flower—5 pieces, each 3 inches long
    for 2 medium flowers—10 pieces, each 3 inches
        long and 10 pieces, each 4 inches long
    for large flower—3 pieces, each 3 inches long and
        14 pieces, each 5 inches long
5 pieces #28 green-covered wire, each 6 inches long

FLOWER ASSEMBLY AND STALK

4 clusters black single craft stamens
green floral tape
1 yard #28 covered wire in color compatible with
    gingham
24-inch piece #20 stem wire, cut as follows:
    for stem—16-inch piece
    for medium flowers—two 2-inch pieces
    for large flower—4-inch piece

Also: wire cutters; toothpicks (to apply glue); découpage or manicure scissors; wax paper or aluminum foil

FLOWER PETALS AND LEAVES

1. For petal shapes for the small flower, take five 3-inch lengths of the #28 covered wire and bend each of them to the shape of Pattern 1. (Diagram A.) Place the middle of your wire at the top of the pattern; shape the wire down on both sides and twist them together at the bottom. Do not cut off wire—it is your petal stem.

2. For petal shapes for the medium-size flowers, repeat Step 1, using ten 3-inch lengths of the #28 covered wire bent to the shape of Pattern 1, and ten 4-inch lengths of the same wire bent to the shape of Pattern 2, making 20 petals in all.

3. For petal shapes for the large flower, repeat Step 1, using three 3-inch lengths of the #28 covered wire bent to the shape of Pattern 1, and fourteen 5-inch lengths of the same wire bent to the shape of Pattern 3, making 17 petals in all.

4. For the leaf shapes, repeat Step 1, using five 6-inch lengths of #28 green-covered wire bent to the shape of Pattern 4, to make 5 leaves.

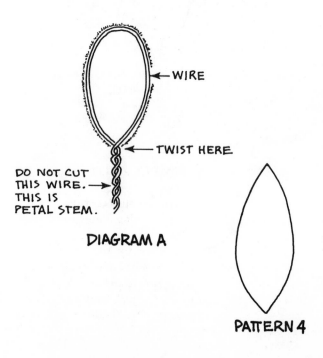

← WIRE

← TWIST HERE

DO NOT CUT THIS WIRE. → THIS IS PETAL STEM.

DIAGRAM A

PATTERN 1   PATTERN 2   PATTERN 3   PATTERN 4

5. Spread out the gingham on a flat surface, right side up. Coat each of your flower petal shapes with glue (do not coat the stems) and place them on the gingham, leaving a little space between them (to make it easier later, when cutting out). Cover with a protective sheet of wax paper or aluminum foil and press flat under a suitable weight. Let dry.

6. Repeat Step 5, using the green burlap ribbon and 5 leaf shapes of green-covered wire.

7. When dry, use découpage scissors to cut each petal and leaf out of the materials and trim off, following closely around the edges of the glued wires. (Diagram B.)

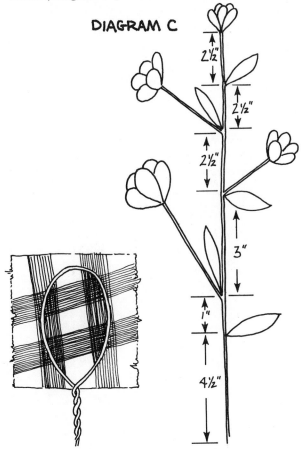

DIAGRAM C

DIAGRAM B

FLOWER ASSEMBLY AND STALK

1. Attach a stamen cluster to one end of the 16-inch length of #20 stem wire, using floral tape. Cut off tape.

2. Take the 5 small petals for the small flowers and use the #28 covered wire to attach them around the stamen cluster, right sides up. Attach them one at a time, overlapping them slightly, wrapping around their stems. Cut off excess wire. Shape the petals by cupping.

3. Begin again with the floral tape, starting just under the small flower, and tape 2½ inches down the stalk. Cut off tape.

4. Attach a stamen cluster to one end of a 2-inch length of #20 stem wire, using floral tape. Cut off tape.

5. For 1 medium-size flower, take 5 small petals and attach them around the stamen cluster as in Step 2 above for small flower. Then attach 5 medium petals just beneath and around them in the same way, placing them so the petal tips are staggered. Cut off wire. Shape the petals by cupping.

6. Repeat Steps 4 and 5 for the second medium-size flower.

7. Start again with the floral tape and tape from just below each medium-size flower down to the end of its stem wire. Cut off tape.

8. For large flower, attach a stamen cluster to one end of the 4-inch length of #20 stem wire, using floral tape. Cut off tape.

9. Repeat Step 5 above as for medium-size flower, using the 3 small petals and the 14 large petals for the large flower.

10. Start again with the floral tape and tape from just below the large flower down to the end of its stem wire. Cut off tape.

FINAL STALK ASSEMBLY

See Diagram C for placement of flowers and leaves.

1. Start again with the floral tape where you left off on the main stalk, 2½ inches below the small flower, attaching 1 leaf at the start. Continue taping another 2½ inches down the stalk.

2. Attach another leaf and a medium-size flower to the stalk. Continue taping another 2½ inches down the stalk.

3. Attach another leaf and the second medium-size flower to the stalk. Continue taping another 3 inches down the stalk.

4. Attach another leaf and the large flower to the stalk. Continue taping 1 inch down the stalk.

5. Attach the last leaf to the stalk. Continue taping down to the end of the stalk. Cut off tape.

THE CREATIVE TOUCH

Cover a container for cutlery and napkins with gingham, then fill one of the compartments with flowers made out of matching gingham. This looks great on a patio table during summertime cookouts. Be sure to buy extra gingham and stitch up some napkins to match.

Iris

Our lifelike iris is made of 6 pale blue silk petals (sized, wired, beautifully highlighted in yellow and dark red), 3 of them with yellow chenille beards. They are taped to a stem and finished by taping, adding 2 (sized and wired) silk leaves and green raffia grasses.

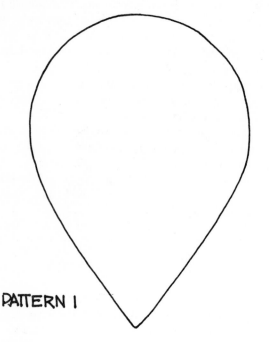

PATTERN 1

MATERIALS FOR 1 FLOWER AND 2 LEAVES

PETALS

1/3 yard pale blue silk lining
sizing formula (page 16)
yellow felt-tip marking pen
dark red oil pencil
deep blue watercolor paint (optional)
6 pieces #28 white-covered wire, each 4 inches long
white resin glue
3 pieces yellow chenille stem, each 2½ inches long

LEAVES

¼ yard dark green silk lining
some sizing (see above)
2 pieces #20 stem wire, each 8 inches long
white resin glue

FLOWER ASSEMBLY AND STEM

15-inch piece #16 stem wire
green floral tape
8 strands dark green raffia, each 15 inches long

Also: pencil, tissue paper, scissors; wire cutters; sponge brush or cosmetics sponge (to apply sizing);

tweezers, toothpicks, wax paper or aluminum foil (for gluing); small artist's paintbrush (for watercolor paint, optional); knitting needle (for veining)

PETALS

1. Make tissue paper Pattern 1, tracing from book pattern. Cut 6 petals out of the pale blue silk lining from Pattern 1.
2. Apply sizing to petals. Set aside to dry.
3. When dry, highlight the petals with the yellow felt-tip pen as shown by the shaded areas in Diagram

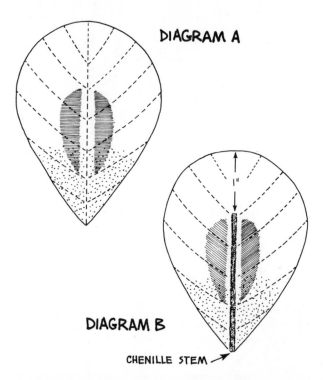

DIAGRAM A

DIAGRAM B

CHENILLE STEM →

A. Set aside to dry. When dry, dot the petals with the red oil pencil, as shown by the dots on Diagram A.

4. Highlight the petal edges with deep blue watercolor paint (optional). Set aside to dry.
5. Take the six 4-inch pieces of #28 white-covered wire and use them to wire each of the highlighted petals on the wrong side. Set aside to dry.
6. Glue one of the yellow chenille stem pieces to the right side of 1 petal, starting 1 inch from the tip and centering it over the covered wire on the wrong side. (Diagram B.)
7. Repeat Step 6 with the other 2 chenille stem pieces and 2 of the petals, to make 3 yellow-bearded petals in all.
8. Using the tip of a knitting needle, mark veins on all flower petals, as shown in Diagram A.

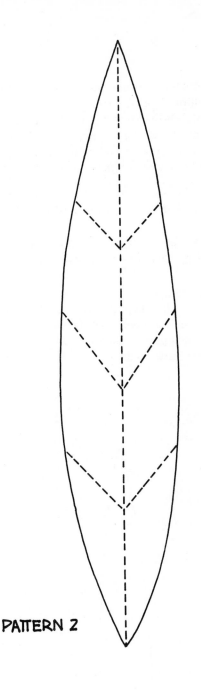

PATTERN 2

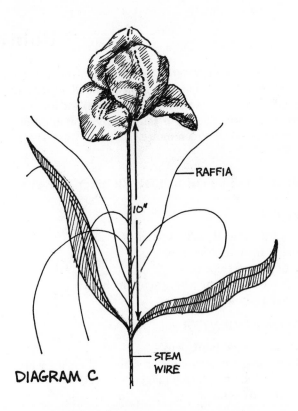

DIAGRAM C

LEAVES

1. Make tissue paper Pattern 2, tracing from book pattern. Cut 4 leaves (to make 2 finished leaves) out of green silk lining from Pattern 2.

2. Apply sizing to leaves. Set aside to dry.

3. Take 2 of the leaves and wire them together with 1 of the 8-inch pieces of #20 stem wire. Set aside to dry.

4. Repeat Step 3 with the other 2 leaves, to make 2 finished leaves in all.

5. Using the tip of a knitting needle, mark veins on leaves as shown by dotted lines in Pattern 2.

FLOWER ASSEMBLY AND STEM

1. Attach the 3 beardless petals around one end of the #16 stem wire, using floral tape. Attach them one at a time, slightly overlapping, with wired sides facing in, as shown in Diagram C.

2. With the floral tape, attach the 3 bearded petals to the stem wire just below the first petals, with the chenille-wired sides facing out. Attach them one at a time, slightly overlapping, and with petal tips staggered to those above.

3. Continue taping 10 inches down the stem wire, taping in a strand of green raffia here and there.

4. Attach the 2 leaves to the stem opposite each other, together with the remaining strands of green raffia. Continue taping down to the end of the stem. Cut off tape.

5. Shape the 3 unbearded petals by cupping up and inward to the center. Shape the 3 bearded petals by cupping outward, then bending each petal outward and down, as shown in Diagram C.

THE CREATIVE TOUCH

We like to make iris in the myriad colors the real flower comes in, ranging from deep purple to yellow to berry brown to white. Our favorite spring bouquet is iris combined with Daffodils (page 38) and some sprigs of Pussy Willow (page 145). Nothing could be brighter after a long, cold winter.

Rubrum Lily

Sheer organza petals (sized, beautifully highlighted and wired) are assembled around a group of peps (some with magenta velvet heads) and attached to stem wire. The lily is finished by taping, adding wired leaves of green moiré.

MATERIALS FOR 1 FLOWER AND 3 LEAVES

PETALS

⅛ yard off-white silk organza
sizing formula (page 16)
set of watercolor paints
6 pieces #22 stem wire, each 5 inches long
white resin glue

FLOWER CENTER

6 white single craft peps
4-inch piece magenta velvet ribbon, 2 inches wide
 (or 2 x 4-inch piece magenta velvet)
clear craft cement

LEAVES

½ yard green moiré ribbon, 1 inch wide
3 pieces #22 stem wire, each 7 inches long
white resin glue

FLOWER ASSEMBLY AND STEM

15-inch piece #18 stem wire
green floral tape

Also: pencil, tissue paper, scissors; wire cutters; sponge brush or cosmetics sponge (to apply sizing); small artist's paintbrush and tiny artist's paintbrush with very few bristles (for highlighting); tweezers, toothpicks, wax paper or aluminum foil (for gluing); knitting needle (for veining)

PETALS

1. Make tissue paper Pattern 1, tracing from book pattern. Cut 6 petals out of the organza from Pattern 1.
2. Apply sizing to the petals. Set aside to dry.
3. When dry, highlight the base of all petals with pale lime green watercolor, using the small artist's paintbrush. Then paint a line of medium pink down the center. Set aside to dry.

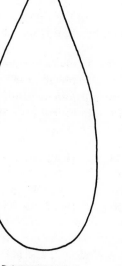

PATTERN 1   PATTERN 2   PATTERN 3

4. Then, using the tiny artist's paintbrush, put dots of magenta watercolor all over each petal, working with a fairly dry brush and using only the tip. Set aside to dry.

5. Take the six 5-inch pieces of #22 stem wire and, using the white resin glue, wire each of the highlighted petals on the wrong side.

6. Using the tip of a knitting needle, vein the petals slightly.

FLOWER CENTER

1. Cut off the heads of 5 peps (leaving 1 pep intact). Reserve the 5 pep stems (discard the heads).

2. Make tissue paper Pattern 2, tracing from book pattern. Cut 5 pep heads out of the magenta velvet ribbon from Pattern 2.

3. Now glue a velvet pep head to the top of each headless pep stem: put a drop of clear craft cement on the wrong side of the velvet pep and set it across the top of the stem, as shown in Diagram A. Hold the pep in position on top of the stem for a minute until set.

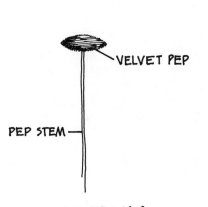

DIAGRAM A

LEAVES

1. Make tissue paper Pattern 3, tracing from book pattern. Cut 3 leaves out of moiré ribbon from Pattern 3.

2. Take the three 7-inch pieces of #22 stem wire and use them to wire each of the moiré leaves on the wrong side.

3. Using the tip of a knitting needle, mark veins on leaves.

FLOWER ASSEMBLY AND STEM

1. Attach the 6 peps to one end of the 15-inch piece of #18 stem wire, using floral tape. The pep with its own head should be centered, with the velvet peps around it. (Diagram B.)

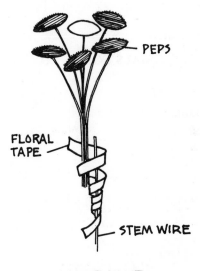

DIAGRAM B

2. Tape the 6 petals around the peps. Tape petals one at a time, overlapping them slightly. Continue taping 5 inches down the stem wire.

3. Attach the first leaf to the stem with the tape. Continue taping another inch down the stem.

4. Attach the second leaf to the stem opposite the first. Continue taping another inch down the stem.

5. Attach the third leaf to the stem on the same side as the first. Continue taping down to the end of the stem. Cut off tape.

6. Shape the petals by cupping.

THE CREATIVE TOUCH

Several of these lilies in a cranberry glass decanter or bud vase provides an elegant accent for a guest bedroom.

51

Poppy

The petals of this imaginative poppy are made of burlap threads. Lengthwise threads are drawn out of a piece of burlap, leaving crosswise threads which are folded over to form loopy petals. Petals are glued around the flower center (drawn threads of a contrasting color) attached to stem wire, the flower and stem finished by taping.

Note: Two colors of burlap will provide contrasting petals and centers to make more than 1 flower, if you wish.

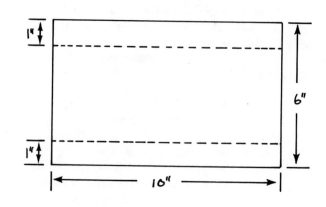

DIAGRAM A

MATERIALS FOR 1 FLOWER

PETAL UNITS

¼ yard burlap in desired color
tacky glue

FLOWER CENTER

¼ yard burlap in contrasting color

FLOWER ASSEMBLY AND STEM

12-inch piece #18 stem wire
tacky glue
green floral tape

Also: ruler, pencil, scissors; wire cutters

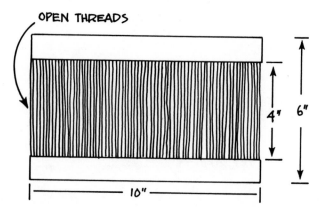

DIAGRAM B

OPEN THREADS

PETAL UNITS

1. With ruler and pencil, mark a 6 x 10-inch oblong on your piece of burlap. Mark a line across the length 1 inch from the top and another line 1 inch from the bottom. (Diagram A.)

2. Cut out the oblong, following the outside lines. This is your petal unit.

3. Draw out 2 lengthwise threads at the ruled line 1 inch from the top, and continue drawing out all the lengthwise threads until you reach the ruled line 1 inch from the bottom. Your burlap piece will now have a 1-inch solid border top and bottom, with only short, crosswise threads left between them, as shown in Diagram B. (Save the drawn threads for the center of a poppy of another color.)

4. Fold the burlap in half lengthwise and glue the edges together along the solid 1-inch borders. The folded threads now form loops that will be the petals. (Diagram C.)

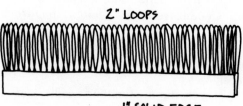

DIAGRAM C

2" LOOPS

1" SOLID EDGE

FLOWER CENTER

1. Repeat Steps 1 to 3 for the petal unit on your piece of contrasting color burlap.

2. Take the drawn threads only and cut them to 4½ inches. (Save the rest of your burlap piece for the petals of another poppy.)

FLOWER ASSEMBLY AND STEM

1. Hold the 4½-inch threads for the flower center in an even bunch and hook one end of the #18 stem wire around the middle. Twist the hook around the wire to secure, and fan out the petals as shown in Diagram D.

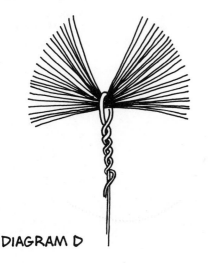

DIAGRAM D

2. Take the petal unit and spread a thin line of glue along one side of the solid 1-inch border. Place the flower center at one end, with the twisted hook lying on the border, and roll it up into the petal unit tightly. (Diagram E.)

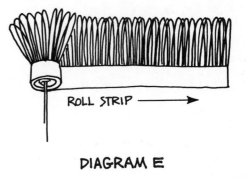

ROLL STRIP ⟶

DIAGRAM E

3. Secure the base of the flower to the stem with floral tape. Continue taping down to the bottom of the stem. Cut off tape.

THE CREATIVE TOUCH

Arrange several of these poppies in a workman's lunch pail planted with a vinca vine or some other cascading greenery.

Powder Puff

Another informal flower made of burlap. The petals are formed of many burlap threads bound in the middle around a flower center (of ball fringe) and attached to the stem wire. It is finished by taping, adding 2 (wired, glued, cut-out) burlap leaves.

Note: The number of threads you use depends on the size of the flower you want to make. And remember that if you have leftover drawn threads from the Poppy (page 52), this is the place to use them.

MATERIALS FOR 1 FLOWER AND 2 LEAVES

PETALS

60 to 100 burlap threads in desired color, cut 4½ inches long

FLOWER CENTER

8-inch piece #20 stem wire
½-inch-diameter ball (from ball fringe) in contrasting color to burlap
green floral tape

LEAVES

2 pieces #28 green-covered wire, each 8 inches long
tacky glue
4-inch square green burlap

FLOWER ASSEMBLY AND STEM

#32 spool wire
green floral tape

Also: scissors; wire cutters; toothpicks, wax paper or aluminum foil (for gluing); découpage or manicure scissors

FLOWER CENTER

1. Bend one end of the #20 stem wire and push it through the middle of the little ball. Bend the end of the wire down to form a small hook and twist it around the stem wire underneath. (Diagram A.)

2. Secure the ball to the stem wire with a bit of floral tape. Cut off tape.

LEAVES

1. Bend each of the two 8-inch lengths of #28 covered wire to the shape of Pattern 1. These are your leaf shapes. (Diagram B.) Place the middle of your wire at the top of the pattern, shape the wire down on both sides, and twist them together at the bottom. Do not cut off wire—it is your leaf stem.

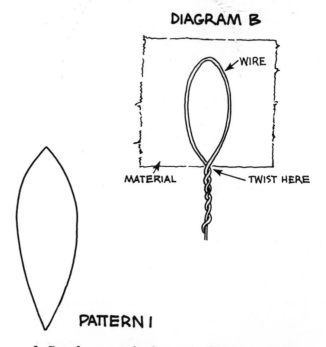

DIAGRAM B

WIRE

MATERIAL — TWIST HERE

PATTERN 1

2. Put the green burlap on a flat surface. Coat each of your leaf shapes with glue (do not coat the stems) and place them on the burlap. Cover with a protective sheet of wax paper or aluminum foil and press flat under a suitable weight. Let dry.

3. When dry, use découpage scissors to cut each leaf out of the burlap and trim off, following closely around the edges of the glued wire.

FLOWER ASSEMBLY AND STEM

1. Hold your burlap threads together in a big bunch and push the stem wire right down through the

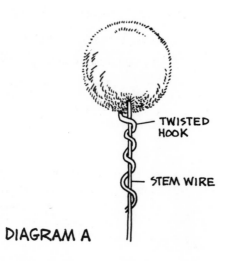

TWISTED HOOK

STEM WIRE

DIAGRAM A

middle till the flower center rests against the threads. (Diagram C.)

2. Use a bit of #32 spool wire to secure the threads tightly around and underneath the flower center to the stem. (Diagram D.) Cut off the spool wire.

3. Using floral tape, start taping at the bottom of the flower, covering the spool wire. Continue taping 3 inches down the stem.

4. Attach the first leaf to the stem with the tape. Continue taping another 2 inches down the stem.

5. Attach the second leaf to the stem opposite the first leaf. Continue taping down to the bottom of the stem. Cut off tape.

THE CREATIVE TOUCH

In spite of its name, this flower looks at home in a den or family room. Put several powder puffs in a tall fireplace matchbox and set on the hearth. Or omit the leaves entirely and arrange the flowers with an assortment of dried weeds.

DIAGRAM C

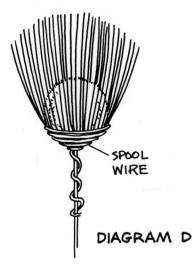

SPOOL WIRE

DIAGRAM D

Rose

This beauty is made of 6 petal units (sized and highlighted) drawn up around a cluster of craft stamens wired to a stem with a calyx taped on underneath. The bud unit is wrapped around a cotton ball and taped to a stem, adding a craft leaf. The rose is finished by taping down the stem, adding the bud stem and 9 craft leaves.

MATERIALS FOR 1 FLOWER, 1 BUD AND 10 LEAVES

PETAL UNITS

¼ yard silk lining (or Sibonne lining) in desired color
sizing formula (page 16)
yellow acrylic paint

FLOWER CENTER

20 yellow single craft stamens
12-inch piece #18 stem wire
#28 spool wire

BUD ASSEMBLY AND STEM

small piece of the silk lining
white resin glue
absorbent cotton cosmetic ball
8-inch piece #20 stem wire
green floral tape
1 medium-size craft leaf (rose type)

FLOWER ASSEMBLY AND STEM

1 large craft calyx (rose type)
white resin glue
green floral tape
9 large craft leaves (rose type)

Also: pencil, tissue paper, scissors; sponge brush or cosmetics sponge (to apply sizing); small artist's paintbrush, yellow felt-tip pen (for highlighting); wire cutters; toothpicks (for gluing); wax paper or aluminum foil (for sizing and gluing)

PETAL UNITS

1. Make tissue paper Patterns 1, 2 and 3, tracing from book patterns. Cut 2 petal units out of your silk lining from each pattern, making 6 petal units in all.
2. Apply sizing to all petal units. Set aside to dry.
3. When dry, highlight the center of 1 of the small petal units with yellow acrylic paint thinned slightly with water, using an almost-dry brush.
4. Shape the petals by cupping and curling.

PATTERN 2

PATTERN 1

FLOWER CENTER

Attach stamens around one end of the #18 stem wire, wrapping with a bit of #28 spool wire, then cut off wire very close.

BUD ASSEMBLY AND STEM

1. Make tissue paper Pattern 4, tracing from book pattern. Cut bud out of your silk lining from Pattern 4.
2. Fold bud piece along horizontal dotted line, then fold again along vertical dotted line. Secure with a dot of glue.

3. With the long fold at the top, wrap the bud piece around the cotton ball, securing at the end with a dot of glue. It will form a slight cone.
4. Dip one end of the #20 stem wire into glue and push it up into the bottom of the cotton ball. Take the floral tape and secure the bud to the stem wire. Continue building up the base of the bud as shown by the shaded area in Diagram A. Then continue taping down the stem for 1 or 2 inches.
5. Attach the medium-size leaf to the stem with the tape. Continue taping down to the bottom of the stem. Cut off tape.

FLOWER ASSEMBLY AND STEM

1. With the tip of your scissors, make a tiny hole in the center of each petal unit.
2. Put the bottom end of the #18 stem wire down through the hole in the highlighted small petal unit

PATTERN 3

and push the unit up the stem until it is right under the stamens. Repeat with the second small petal unit, turning it so petal tips are staggered to those above.

3. Repeat with the 2 medium-size petal units, then with the 2 large petal units, staggering placement of petal tips with each row.

4. Push the calyx up the stem wire right under the petals, securing with a dot of glue.

5. Start at the top with floral tape and tape 3 inches down the stem wire.

6. Attach the bud stem to the main stem with the tape. Continue taping another 2 inches down the stem.

7. Attach a leaf to the stem opposite the bud. Continue taping down the stem.

8. Add the rest of the leaves, one at a time, placing them as desired, and finish taping down to the bottom of the stem. Cut off tape.

9. Highlight the edges of the large petals with the yellow felt-tip pen.

THE CREATIVE TOUCH

Perfection equals this rose displayed all alone in your favorite silver or crystal bud vase.

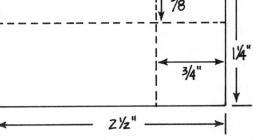

PATTERN 4

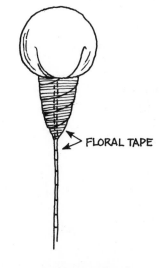

FLORAL TAPE

DIAGRAM A

Cabbage Rose

This full-blown rose consists of 20 small and large petals (sized, wired, highlighted) and a flower center (a tiny cotton ball covered with a bit of fabric). Petals and storebought stamens are assembled around the center and taped to the stem. The flower base is built up with floral tape, then the stem is inserted into green velvet tubing and finished with a bud (made like the flower) and 4 craft leaves.

Note: Green velvet tubing is available at fabric and trimmings stores. Note also that the stem may be finished by taping, if you prefer.

MATERIALS FOR 1 FLOWER, 1 BUD AND 4 LEAVES

FLOWER AND BUD PETALS

¼ yard silk lining in desired color
sizing formula (page 16)
12 pieces #22 stem wire, each 5 inches long
white resin glue
brown oil pencil

FLOWER AND BUD CENTERS

2 pieces black silk, each 3 inches square (or 2 scraps
    of nylon hose and black commercial dye)
absorbent cotton cosmetics ball divided in half
#32 spool wire

LEAVES

4 large craft leaves (chrysanthemum type)
white acrylic spray paint (flat finish)

BUD ASSEMBLY AND STEM

10-inch piece #16 stem wire
#32 spool wire
white resin glue
green floral tape
10-inch piece green velvet tubing (or green floral
    tape)

FLOWER ASSEMBLY AND STEM

18-inch piece #16 stem wire
20 white single craft stamens
#32 spool wire
white resin glue
green floral tape
18-inch piece green velvet tubing (or green floral
    tape)

Also: pencil, tissue paper, scissors; sponge brush or cosmetics sponge (to apply sizing); wire cutters; newspaper, tweezers, toothpicks, wax paper or aluminum foil (for gluing); découpage or manicure scissors.

FLOWER AND BUD PETALS

1. Make tissue paper Patterns 1 and 2, tracing from book patterns. Cut 8 small petals out of your silk lining from Pattern 1, and 12 large petals from Pattern 2, making 20 petals for the flower.

2. Cut 1 small petal out of the silk lining from Pattern 1 for the bud.

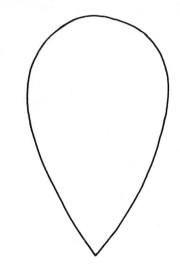

PATTERN I

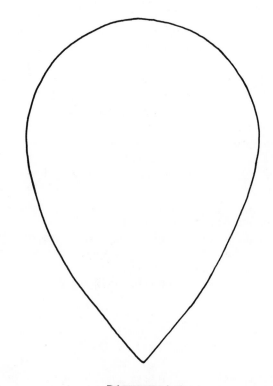

PATTERN 2

3. Make tissue paper Pattern 3, tracing from book pattern. Cut 12 pieces out of the silk lining from Pattern 3, making 12 petal wire coverings.

PETAL WIRE COVERING

PATTERN 3

4. Apply sizing to all petals and petal wire coverings. Set aside to dry.

5. Wire the 12 large petals with the 12 pieces of #22 stem wire. Let dry.

6. Lightly glue the 12 petal wire coverings over each of the exposed petal wires, as shown in Diagram A.

7. Turn all petals right side up and highlight them with the oil pencil, as shown in the shaded area of Diagram B.

8. Shape all petals by cupping and curling.

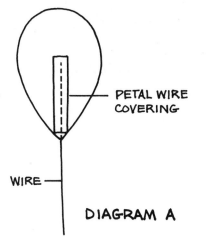

DIAGRAM A

DIAGRAM B

FLOWER AND BUD CENTERS

1. Have cut and ready the 2 squares of black silk. (Or dye 2 scraps of nylon hose with commercial liquid dye, following package directions. Let dry thoroughly.)

2. Divide the absorbent cotton ball into 2 small balls. Cover 1 ball smoothly with the black silk, drawing the fabric together underneath. (Diagram C.) Secure it around tightly with a bit of #32 spool wire, but do not cut the wire off the spool. Trim off excess fabric, leaving ¼ inch of fabric below wire. This is your bud center.

3. Repeat Step 2 later with the second small ball to make the flower center, again leaving the #32 spool wire attached.

DIAGRAM C

LEAVES

1. Spread some newspaper on a flat surface and put the craft leaves on it, right side up.

2. Mist the leaves *very* lightly with 1 coat of white spray paint so the green leaf color becomes slightly gray. Set aside to dry.

BUD ASSEMBLY AND STEM

1. Push one end of the 10-inch piece of #16 stem wire up into the bottom of the bud center. Secure by wrapping around with the #32 spool wire that's still attached to the bud center, then cut off the wire very close.

2. Take the small petal reserved for the bud and wrap it around the bud center, securing with a dot of glue.

3. Using the floral tape, cover the base of the bud, building up the stem under the bud just slightly. Cut off the tape.

4. Very lightly glue down the length of the stem wire. Take the 10-inch piece of green velvet tubing

59

and push the stem wire down into it so it is entirely covered.

5. Using découpage scissors, cut a small hole in the tubing near the bud, where a leaf will be placed.

6. Lightly coat a leaf stem with glue and insert it into the hole in the tubing, pushing it down so no stem shows.

FLOWER ASSEMBLY AND STEM

1. Push one end of the 18-inch piece of #16 stem wire up into the bottom of the flower center.

2. Secure the stamens around the flower center, wrapping around tightly with the #32 spool wire that's still attached to the flower center. Do not cut off the wire. (Diagram D.)

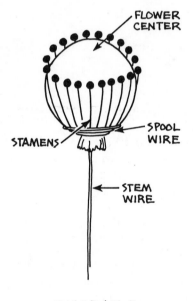

DIAGRAM D

3. Attach 4 of the small petals around the stamens, spacing them evenly and wrapping tightly with the spool wire. Do not cut off the wire.

4. Using the remaining small petals, attach them in a second row, placing so petal tips are staggered. Do not cut off the wire.

5. Attach 6 of the large petals around in the same way, with petal tips staggered. Do not cut off the wire.

6. Attach the remaining 6 petals around in the same way, again staggering the petal tips. Now cut off the spool wire very close.

7. With the floral tape, build up the stem directly under the last petal row, as shown by the shaded area in Diagram E. Cut off the tape.

8. Very lightly glue down the length of the stem wire.

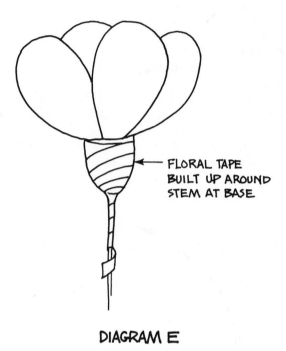

FLORAL TAPE BUILT UP AROUND STEM AT BASE

DIAGRAM E

9. Take the 18-inch piece of green velvet tubing and push the stem wire down into it so it is completely covered.

10. Using découpage scissors, cut 3 small holes in the tubing where you want the remaining leaves to be. Lightly coat the 3 leaf stems with glue and insert them into the 3 holes, pushing them down so no stems show.

11. Join the velvet bud stem to the main stem by twisting them together.

THE CREATIVE TOUCH

These dramatic roses are beautifully set off in a silver or crystal wine cooler or vase. If you use crystal, see page 151 for instructions on supporting the flowers and creating an artificial waterline.

Cabbage Rose Centerpiece

Very easy, very pretty. Successive rows of (sized) organza petals are glued around the outside of a brandy snifter. The base is slipcovered in green felt—and a candle is inserted for a lovely glow. A bud and 2 felt leaves may be added at the base.

MATERIALS FOR 1 CENTERPIECE

PETALS

brandy snifter 6 to 8 inches tall
½ yard cotton organza in desired color
sizing formula (page 16)

BASE

¼ yard green felt
white resin glue

CENTERPIECE ASSEMBLY

white resin glue
large fat candle, about 4 inches tall

BUD AND 2 LEAVES (OPTIONAL)

a bit of the cotton organza
sizing formula (see above)
a bit of the green felt
white resin glue
12-inch piece #16 stem wire
green floral tape
12 inches green satin ribbon, ½ inch wide

Also: pencil, tissue paper, scissors; sponge brush or cosmetics sponge, wax paper or aluminum foil (to apply sizing); compass, wire cutters (if making bud)

PETALS

1. Make tissue paper Pattern 1, tracing from book pattern. Cut approximately 50 petals out of organza from Pattern 1—you'll need more or fewer petals, depending on the size of your snifter.
2. Apply sizing to the petals. Set aside to dry.
3. When dry, shape petals by curling. (See photograph on page 41.)

BASE

1. Measure the diameter of the base of your snifter.
2. With a compass, draw 2 circles on the green felt, each circle ⅛ inch wider in diameter than the snifter base. Cut out the 2 circles.
3. Take 1 circle and cut a slit across the diameter not quite to the edges.
4. Glue the 2 circles together around the edges only. Set aside to dry.

CENTERPIECE ASSEMBLY

1. Starting at the top of your snifter, glue a row of overlapping petals around the outside of the glass so the tips come just a little above the rim. Glue only the base of the petals, so the tips are free. Set aside to dry.
2. Glue a second row ½ inch below the first, making sure to stagger the petal tips. Let dry and glue on successive rows right down to the bottom of the snifter bowl. Allow each row to dry before gluing on

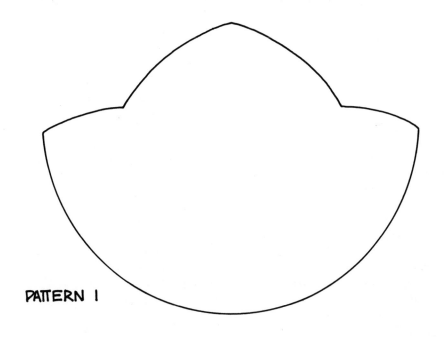

PATTERN 1

the next and be sure to stagger the petal tips each time.

3. Slip the snifter base through the slit into its green felt cover.

4. Melt a few drops of wax from your candle into the bottom of the snifter. Press the candle base into the melted wax so it's level and centered. Light when ready.

BUD AND 2 LEAVES (OPTIONAL)

1. Make tissue paper Pattern 2, tracing from book pattern. Cut 1 bud petal out of organza from Pattern 2.

2. Apply sizing to the bud petal. Set aside to dry.

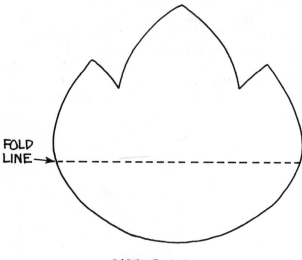

FOLD LINE →

PATTERN 2

3. Make tissue paper Pattern 3, tracing from book pattern. Cut 2 leaves out of green felt from Pattern 3.

4. Fold the bud petal toward you along the dotted line shown in Pattern 2.

PATTERN 3

5. Roll bud petal edges inward from both ends until they touch, following direction of arrows in Diagram A, and secure with a tiny bit of glue.

6. Push the end of the piece of #16 stem wire up into the bottom of the bud and attach with floral tape.

7. With the tape, attach the 2 leaves to the stem right under and around the bud and continue taping down to the bottom of the stem. Cut off tape.

8. Cover the stem by winding with the satin ribbon, securing at the ends with a drop of glue.

9. Wrap the lower part of the bud stem around the stem of the brandy snifter right under the bowl.

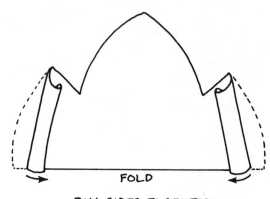

FOLD

ROLL SIDES TO CENTER

DIAGRAM A

THE CREATIVE TOUCH

These cabbage rose centerpieces decorated the tables at the reception of one of the more memorable weddings in our town. The bride's aunts made them weeks in advance of the big day—can you imagine anything nicer to do for a bride you know?

We also recommend this centerpiece for a church or school benefit bridge table prize. It's the perfect project to make in quantity, using the assembly-line technique.

Rose Pin

This graceful silk rose is composed of 5 petal units in two shades of color, with a small velvet petal unit to add depth. Petal units are drawn up around a stamen cluster taped to a stem; the stem is inserted into green velvet tubing and finished by adding 3 leaves. The finished rose is then wired to a storebought bar-pin back.

MATERIALS FOR 1 FLOWER, 3 LEAVES AND A PIN

PETAL UNITS

¼ yard medium-colored silk lining
¼ yard light-colored silk lining
3 x 6-inch piece velvet in matching medium color
sizing formula (page 16)

FLOWER ASSEMBLY AND STEM

cluster of yellow single craft stamens
3-inch piece #16 stem wire
green floral tape
clear craft cement
craft calyx (rose type)
3-inch piece green velvet tubing
3 small velvet craft leaves (rose type)
white resin glue

PIN ASSEMBLY

1-inch jewelry bar-pin back
#32 spool wire

Also: pencil, tissue paper, scissors; sponge brush or cosmetics sponge (to apply sizing); découpage or manicure scissors; tweezers, toothpick (for gluing); wax paper or aluminum foil (for gluing and sizing); wire cutters

PETAL UNITS

1. Make tissue paper Patterns 1 and 2, tracing from book patterns. Cut out of medium-colored silk 2 small petal units from Pattern 1. Cut out of light-colored silk 1 small petal unit from Pattern 1, and 2 large petal units from Pattern 2.

2. Make tissue paper Pattern 3, tracing from book pattern. Cut 1 half-petal unit out of velvet from Pattern 3.

3. Apply sizing to silk petal units (not velvet). Set aside to dry.

FLOWER ASSEMBLY AND STEM

1. Attach stamen cluster to the end of the piece of #16 stem wire, using green floral tape. Cut off tape.

2. With the tip of your scissors, make a tiny hole in the exact center of each of the silk petal units.

PATTERN 1

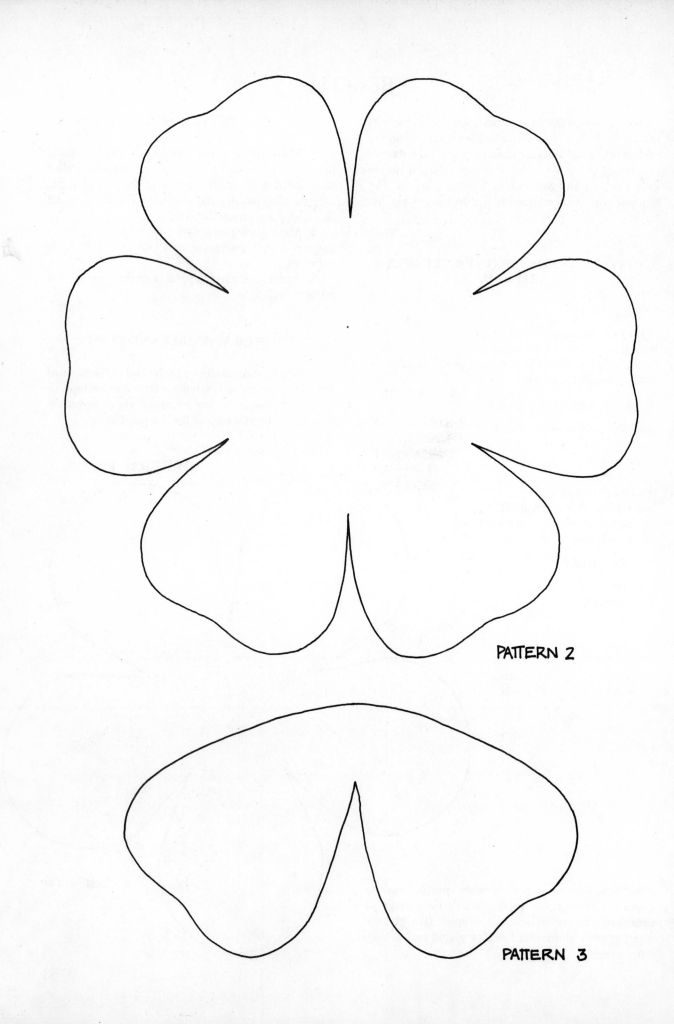

PATTERN 2

PATTERN 3

TOP, LEFT TO RIGHT: *powder puffs; poppies.*
CENTER: *anemones; rose pin; gingham flower stalk.*
BOTTOM: *bachelor's buttons; rambler roses;*
bridal bouquet; evening corsage.
PHOTOGRAPHS: *Otto Maya.*

(At right)
Top, LEFT TO RIGHT: *oriental fruit blossom branch; tulips.*
BOTTOM: *silk rose; strawberry basket; rubrum lilies; cabbage rose centerpiece; cyclamen plant.*

(At left)
TOP: *artichoke wreath.*
CENTER: *seashell wreath.*
BOTTOM: *miniature seashell bouquet; miniature rosebuds; tea rose flowers.*

TOP: *feathery flowers and cattails.*
CENTER: *pompon flowers; artichoke flower bouquet.*
BOTTOM: *seashell flowers #1 & #2 arranged with mushroom*
flowers, pampas grass and coral; pine-cone flowers.

TOP: *fuchsia.*
CENTER: *arrangement of anemones, rubrum lilies, daffodils,
fuchsia, and iris; shaggy zinnias; cabbage roses.*
BOTTOM: *bridesmaid's bouquet; arrangement of daffodils, iris, and
pussy willows; black-eyed Susans.*

TOP: *mod daisy.*
CENTER: *plastic flowers #3; needlepoint flowers.*
BOTTOM: *hibiscus; mountain flowers; French dahlia; plastic flowers #1.*

(At left)

TOP, LEFT TO RIGHT: *three-dimensional poppy picture; giant rose.*
BOTTOM: *papier-mâché posies; carnations; daisies.*

(At right)

TOP, LEFT TO RIGHT: *rickrack flowers; denim flowers; poinsettia.*
BOTTOM: *fantasy flowers; desert flowers on a rock; chrysanthemum; fluffy carnations; rickrack flowers.*

Top: *oriental poppies.*
Center: *cornhusk flowers; yarn flowers; egg carton rose.*
Bottom: *mayblossoms; pansy pin; fish-scale flower pin;*
forget-me-nots.

Top: *plastic flowers #2.*
Center: *miniature iris; party favor flower; cactus flower.*
Bottom: *dollhouse flowers; jewelry flowers; Pendo flower
necklace; jewelry flowers.*

3. Push the stem wire down through the holes of the 2 small medium-colored petal units and push them up the stem until they are right under the stamen cluster. Make sure to turn them so petal tips are staggered.

4. Take the velvet half-petal unit, right side up, and apply a small amount of clear craft cement to the base. Press it up against the underside of the petal unit above it, staggering the petal tips, as shown in Diagram A.

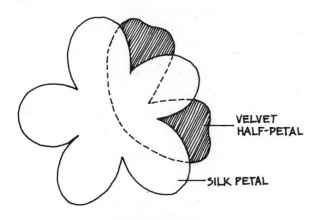

DIAGRAM A

5. Put the stem wire down through the hole of the small light-colored petal unit and push it up the stem just under the velvet, staggering the petal tips. Add a tiny bit of clear craft cement to the base and press it up against the underside of the velvet piece to secure.

6. Put the stem wire down through the holes of the 2 large light-colored petal units and push them up the stem, again staggering petal tips for both.

7. Put a dot of clear craft cement inside the calyx. Push the stem wire down through the hole, and push the calyx up the stem close under the petals.

8. Lightly glue down the length of the stem wire. Take the piece of green velvet tubing and push the stem wire down into it so it is entirely covered.

9. Using découpage scissors, cut 3 small holes in the tubing where the leaves will be placed.

10. Lightly coat the 3 leaf stems with white resin glue. One at a time, insert each stem into a hole in the tubing, pushing it down so no stem shows.

PIN ASSEMBLY

Attach the flower stem to the bar-pin back with #32 spool wire, passing the wire through the holes in the bar pin and wrapping it around and around, as shown in Diagram B. Be sure to place pin-back so it is hidden by the flower.

THE CREATIVE TOUCH

Pin this stunning accessory to your prettiest blouse or dress for a romantic night on the town.

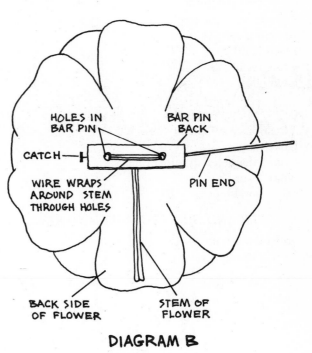

DIAGRAM B

Rambler Rose

This is composed of many rows of silk petals glued around craft stamens taped to a stem. Green silk calyx petals are glued around underneath them and the stem is finished by taping, adding in a bud (silk petals and calyx glued around a styrofoam ball and taped to a stem) and craft leaves.

Easy as it is, it does take time to make, but the result is worthy of being an heirloom.

MATERIALS FOR 1 FLOWER, 1 BUD AND 4 LEAVES

FLOWER AND BUD PETALS AND CALYXES

¼ yard silk in desired color (or ¼ yard white silk and commercial liquid dye)
4-inch-square piece green silk

FLOWER ASSEMBLY

3 single craft stamens
10-inch piece #18 stem wire
green floral tape
white resin glue
tacky glue

BUD ASSEMBLY

4-inch piece #20 stem wire
tacky glue
¾-inch-diameter styrofoam ball
white resin glue
green floral tape

FLOWER AND BUD ASSEMBLY AND STEM

green floral tape
4 craft leaves (rose type)

Also: pencil, tissue paper, scissors; wire cutters; toothpicks (for gluing)

FLOWER AND BUD PETALS AND CALYXES

1. Make tissue paper Patterns 1, 2, 3 and 4, tracing from book patterns. Cut out of your colored silk: 6 inner petals from Pattern 1; 6 small petals from Pattern 2; 6 medium-size petals from Pattern 3; and 24 large petals from Pattern 4. (If you have white silk, tint it with the commercial liquid dye, following package directions, then cut out petals.)

2. Make tissue paper Pattern 5, tracing from book pattern. Cut 12 calyx petals out of green silk from Pattern 5.

3. Shape petals from Patterns 2, 3 and 4 by cupping.

FLOWER ASSEMBLY

1. Attach the stamens to the end of the piece of #18 stem wire, using green floral tape. Cut off tape.

2. Take the 6 inner silk petals cut from Pattern 1, fold them in half lengthwise, and crease with your nail along the fold (shown by dotted line on the pattern). Put a drop of white resin glue on the pointed end of each petal and glue them to the top of the stem wire, placing them around the stamens with petals overlapping slightly.

3. Take the 6 small silk petals cut from Pattern 2, put a drop of tacky glue on the pointed end of each petal, and glue them around the stem wire just below the folded petals, overlapping them slightly and making sure petal tips are staggered.

4. Repeat Step 3 with the 6 medium-size silk petals cut from Pattern 3.

5. Repeat Step 3 with 6 of the large petals cut from Pattern 4. Then repeat Step 3 twice more, using 6 large petals cut from Pattern 4 each time.

FOLD LINE

PATTERN 1   PATTERN 2   PATTERN 3   PATTERN 4   PATTERN 5

6. Take 6 of the green silk calyx petals cut from Pattern 5, put a drop of tacky glue on the pointed end of each, and glue them one at a time around the stem wire, close under the petals, overlapping them slightly.

7. To prevent petals from fraying, use a toothpick and apply white resin glue very lightly around the edges.

BUD ASSEMBLY

1. Dip the end of the piece of #20 stem wire into tacky glue. Then push the glued end up into the center of the styrofoam ball. Let dry.

2. Take 6 of the large silk petals cut from Pattern 4, put a little white resin glue on the base of each, and glue them one at a time around the styrofoam ball, overlapping the petals slightly.

3. Take 6 of the green silk calyx petals cut from Pattern 5, put a drop of tacky glue on the pointed end of each, and glue them one at a time around the base of the ball under the petals, overlapping them slightly.

4. Using the floral tape, tape from the top of the stem down to the bottom. Cut off tape.

FLOWER AND BUD ASSEMBLY AND STEM

1. Take the #18 stem wire with its flower attached and start taping down it with floral tape. Start at the top, securing the bases of the green calyx petals, then continue taping down the stem for 2 inches.

2. Attach a leaf to the stem with the tape. Continue taping another 2 inches down the stem.

3. Attach the bud stem and 1 leaf to the stem opposite the first leaf.

4. Continue taping down to the end of the stem, adding the remaining 2 leaves where desired. Cut off tape.

THE CREATIVE TOUCH

Whether you make a single one or an armful of these absolutely exquisite roses, be sure to keep the container simple so as not to detract from their beauty.

Strawberry Basket

These charming "berries" are painted walnuts, and they're interspersed with organdy flowers (the easy kind, pasted to wire petal shapes, cut out and taped around stamens) and plastic strawberry foliage. They are all arranged in a strawberry box (painted, filled with styrofoam topped with dried moss, and finished with velvet ribbon)—to make a most elegant decorative accessory.

MATERIALS FOR 11 STRAWBERRIES, 10 FLOWERS, FOLIAGE AND BASKET

STRAWBERRIES

11 walnuts
11 short pieces stem wire (optional)
styrofoam block (optional)
red acrylic paint
black acrylic paint
11 craft calyxes (small rose size)
bunch of plastic strawberry foliage
white resin glue
crystal clear acrylic sealer

FLOWER PETAL UNITS

¼ yard white organdy
10 pieces #28 white-covered wire, each 12 inches long
white resin glue

FLOWER ASSEMBLY AND STEM

60 yellow double craft stamens
10 pieces #28 white-covered wire, each 1½ inches long
10 pieces #20 stem wire, each 4 inches long
green floral tape

STRAWBERRY BASKET ASSEMBLY

1-quart wooden berry basket
acrylic spray paint or stain in desired color
24 inches velvet ribbon, ½ inch wide, in desired color
tacky glue
styrofoam
dried sheet moss
bunch of plastic strawberry foliage from above

Also: small artist's paintbrush; pencil, compass, tissue paper; wire cutters; newspaper, tweezers, toothpicks, wax paper or aluminum foil (for spraying and gluing); découpage or manicure scissors

STRAWBERRIES

1. Paint the walnuts with red acrylic paint, using a small artist's paintbrush. Set aside to dry. (We recommend inserting a piece of stem wire into the hole in the base of each walnut shell—you can hold the stem wire while painting the walnut, then stick it into the styrofoam block to dry.)

2. When dry, paint tiny dots on each with black acrylic paint to resemble strawberries. Set aside to dry.

3. Strip flowers from a bunch of plastic strawberry foliage. Reserve foliage; discard the flowers.

4. Put a dot of white resin glue in the centers of the 11 craft calyxes, and glue each one to the broad end of a painted strawberry. (It's not necessary for all strawberries to have calyxes.) Set aside to dry.

5. Put down a protective sheet of newspaper and spray strawberries and the bunch of plastic foliage with crystal clear acrylic spray. Set aside to dry.

FLOWER PETAL UNITS

1. With a compass, draw a circle 1½ inches in diameter on tissue paper. Cut out the circle to make your petal unit pattern.

2. Cut 20 circles out of the white organdy from the pattern.

3. Take 1 piece of the #28 white-covered wire and wrap it around a pencil 5 times to form 5 circles, as shown in Diagram A.

4. Slide the circles off the pencil, twist the ends to secure, and clip off the excess wire. Spread the circles so they lie close together to form 1 large flat circle of petals, as shown in Diagram B. This is a petal unit shape.

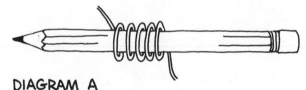

DIAGRAM A

DIAGRAM B

5. Repeat Steps 3 and 4 with the remaining pieces of #28 covered wire to make 10 petal unit shapes in all.

6. Spread 10 of the organdy circles on a flat surface. Dip your wire petal unit shapes into glue and center each one on an organdy circle. With a toothpick, add a little glue to the tops of the wire shapes and center a second organdy circle on top of each, sandwich fashion. Set aside to dry.

7. When dry, use découpage scissors to trim off the excess organdy, following closely around the edges of the glued wire.

8. With the tip of your scissors, make a tiny hole in the exact center of each finished petal unit.

FLOWER ASSEMBLY AND STEM

1. Take 6 stamens and fold them in half. Make a small hook with one end of a piece of the #28 white-covered wire and bind the stamens together. Press hook close to stem below stamens. (Diagram C.)

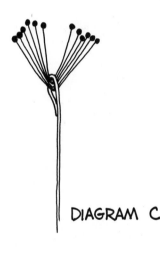

DIAGRAM C

2. Using the floral tape, attach the bound stamens with their hook to the top of a piece of the #20 stem wire. Cut off tape.

3. Repeat Steps 1 and 2 nine more times, making 10 stamen-topped stems in all.

4. Take a petal unit, put a stem wire down through its center hole, and push the petal unit up the stem wire right under the stamens.

5. Secure the petal unit to the stem wire with floral tape, then tape down the stem to the end. Cut off tape.

6. Repeat Steps 4 and 5 with the rest of the petal units and stem wires, making 10 flowers in all.

STRAWBERRY BASKET ASSEMBLY

1. Paint the berry basket with acrylic spray paint (or stain). Set aside to dry.

2. When dry, take the velvet ribbon and glue it around the rim of the basket with tacky glue. Set aside to dry.

3. When dry, cut some styrofoam to fill the inside of the basket up to ½ inch from the top. Cut a piece of dried sheet moss to fit; wet it, then squeeze it out (to make it pliable) and place on top of the styrofoam. Let dry to shape of basket.

4. Arrange the plastic foliage in the basket, sticking the ends down into the styrofoam.

5. Insert the flower stems into the styrofoam and arrange the strawberries among the flowers.

THE CREATIVE TOUCH

This is our favorite housewarming gift; we make it with ribbons on the berry basket to match or accent the décor.

Tulip

Six exquisite silk petals (sized, wired and high-lighted) are taped around storebought stamens attached to a stem wire and finished by taping and adding in 2 silk (sized and wired) leaves.

MATERIALS FOR 1 FLOWER AND 2 LEAVES

PETALS

⅛ yard silk lining in desired color
sizing formula (page 16)
6 pieces #22 stem wire, each 3½ inches long
tacky glue
felt-tip marking pen in pale color (optional)

LEAVES

⅛ yard green silk lining
sizing formula (see above)
2 pieces #22 stem wire, each 8 inches long
white resin glue

FLOWER ASSEMBLY AND STEM

5 black single craft stamens
12-inch piece #16 stem wire
green floral tape
felt-tip marking pen in pale color (optional)

Also: pencil, tissue paper, scissors; wire cutters; sponge brush or cosmetics sponge (to apply sizing); tweezers, toothpicks, wax paper or aluminum foil (for gluing and sizing)

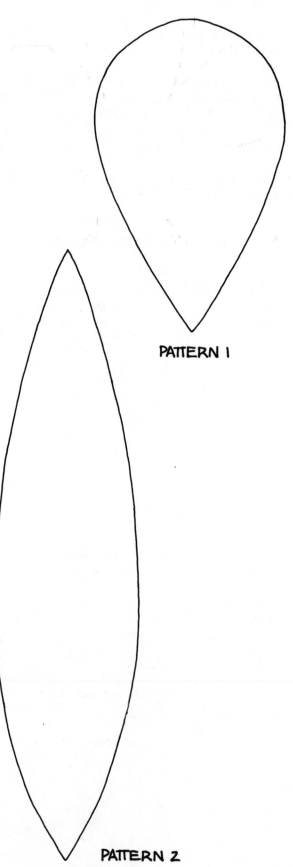

PATTERN 1

PATTERN 2

PETALS

1. Make tissue paper Pattern 1, tracing from book pattern. Cut 12 petals (to make 6 finished petals) out of silk, from Pattern 1.
2. Apply sizing to petals. Set aside to dry.
3. Wire 2 petals sandwich fashion with a 3½-inch piece of the #22 stem wire and glue, making 1 finished petal. Set aside to dry.
4. Repeat Step 3 with the remaining petals and 3½-inch pieces of #22 stem wire, making 6 finished petals in all.
5. Shape the petals by cupping.
6. If you like, you may highlight around the inner centers of the petals, applying the pale color to the pointed petal bases with the felt-tip pen.

LEAVES

1. Make tissue Pattern 2, tracing from book pattern. Cut 4 leaves (to make 2 finished leaves) out of green silk from Pattern 2.

2. Apply sizing to leaves. Set aside to dry.

3. Wire 2 leaves with an 8-inch piece of the #22 stem wire and glue. Set aside to dry.

4. Repeat Step 3 with the remaining 2 leaves, making 2 finished leaves in all.

FLOWER ASSEMBLY AND STEM

1. Attach stamens to the end of the piece of #16 stem wire, using green floral tape.

2. Still using the tape, attach the petals to the stem wire around the stamens. Add them one at a time, overlapping them slightly. When all are attached, continue taping down the stem wire for 8 inches.

3. Attach the leaves to the stem directly opposite each other. Continue taping down the stem to the end. Cut off tape.

4. If you like, you may highlight the tips of the petals, using the felt-tip marking pen.

THE CREATIVE TOUCH

If you plant several of these tulips in a terra-cotta pot, we guarantee that most of your friends will think they are real.

Shaggy Zinnia

Double-layered small, medium and large petals (sized and highlighted) are glued together with the tips staggered, then hooked to the stem wire. A store-bought velvet center is glued on top, and it's finished by taping, adding 2 leaves.

MATERIALS FOR 1 FLOWER AND 2 LEAVES

PETAL UNITS

1/3 yard silk lining in desired color
sizing formula (page 16)
tacky glue
watercolor paints (optional)

FLOWER ASSEMBLY AND STEM

10-inch piece #16 stem wire
½-inch-diameter brown velvet craft flower center
white resin glue
green floral tape
2 velvet craft leaves (chrysanthemum type)

Also: pencil, tissue paper, scissors; sponge brush or cosmetics sponge (to apply sizing); toothpicks (to apply glue); wax paper or aluminum foil (for sizing and gluing); small artist's paintbrush (if highlighting); wire cutters

PETAL UNITS

1. Make tissue paper Patterns 1, 2 and 3, tracing from book patterns.

2. Using your silk lining, cut out 2 small petal units from Pattern 1, 2 medium-size units from Pattern 2, and 2 large units from Pattern 3.

3. Apply sizing to petal units. Set aside to dry.

4. When dry, take a small petal unit, put a tiny drop of glue in the center, and cover with a second small unit, placing so petal tips are staggered. Set aside to dry.

5. Repeat Step 4 with 2 medium-size petal units.

6. Repeat Step 4 with 2 large petal units.

7. You may highlight each petal with a watercolor stripe (shown by dotted lines on the patterns), using a small artist's paintbrush.

PATTERN 1

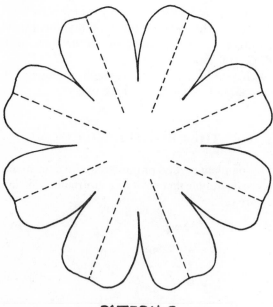

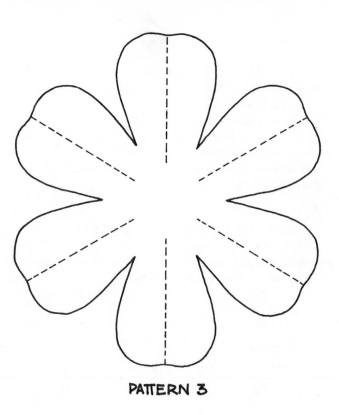

PATTERN 2

PATTERN 3

FLOWER ASSEMBLY AND STEM

1. Place the large petal unit down flat. Center the medium-size unit on it, staggering petal tips. Then do the same with the small unit. Press down with the tip of your scissors in the exact center, making marks through all layers for 2 tiny holes.

2. With the tip of your scissors, cut 2 tiny holes in each petal unit where marked.

3. Make a 2-inch hook at the top of the #16 stem wire. Put the bottom of the wire down through 1 hole in the small petal unit, with the hook end going down through the second hole. Now put the wire and hook through the 2 holes in the medium-size unit and then through the 2 holes in the large unit. Make sure all petal tips are nicely staggered; then twist the hook around the stem wire underneath the petals to secure.

4. Put a little tacky glue on the underside of the velvet flower center and press in place in the top center of the flower, covering the wire. Set aside to dry.

5. With the floral tape, start at the top of the stem wire and tape 2 inches down.

6. Attach the first leaf to the stem. Continue taping another 2 inches down the stem.

7. Attach the second leaf to the stem opposite the first. Continue taping down to the bottom of the stem. Cut off tape.

8. Shape petals by cupping and by curling the tips and edges.

THE CREATIVE TOUCH

Arrange a number of these zinnias in different colors in a soup tureen, then fill in with dried baby's breath.

Flowers from Ribbon and Trim

In recent years a wide range of fancy ribbons and trims have become available to the consumer, a situation that delights us, because ribbons and trims are wonderfully suited to making all kinds of attractive flowers. Keep an eye peeled for sales on ribbons and trims at your local fabric or department store; we often buy short lengths or discontinued colors and patterns for only a few cents a yard. The projects in this chapter also provide the ideal way to use up bits and pieces of ribbon and trim left over from sewing projects.

Since most of these flowers are inexpensive and easy to make, they are perfect gifts for someone in the hospital, for a housewarming, or just to say "thank you." They are also suitable for places where you want a small but lively splash of color, as in a guest room, powder room or sun porch.

Fantasy flower of ribbon, page 79

Chrysanthemum, page 76

Denim flower, page 78

Fluffy Carnation

Pretty and easy—made with 2 small pieces of multi-layered nylon trim. It consists of an inner petal hooked into a stem wire and tightly rolled, with an outer petal shirred around it. A calyx is added, built up with tape, and the stem is finished by taping, adding 3 leaves. A bud and stem may also be added, if desired. Eyelet or lace trim is also very nice for this.

MATERIALS FOR 1 FLOWER AND 3 LEAVES

PETALS

2-inch piece multi-layered nylon trim, 1½ inches wide (with 1 selvedge), in desired color
6-inch piece multi-layered nylon trim, 1½ inches wide, same as above
matching sewing thread

FLOWER ASSEMBLY AND STEM

8-inch piece #20 stem wire
tacky glue
green floral tape
craft calyx (carnation type)
3 craft leaves (carnation type)

BUD AND STEM (OPTIONAL)

2-inch piece same multi-layered nylon trim
3-inch piece #20 stem wire
tacky glue
green floral tape

Also: scissors, sewing needle; toothpicks (to apply glue); wire cutters

PETALS

1. Inner petal: Take the 2-inch piece of trim and, with the tip of your scissors, make a tiny hole just above the selvedge, as shown in Diagram A.

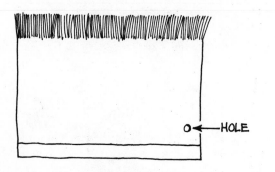

DIAGRAM A

2. Outer petal: Take the 6-inch piece of trim and, with needle and doubled thread, sew a small running stitch along the selvedge, as shown in Diagram B. Do not finish off; set aside as is, needle still attached.

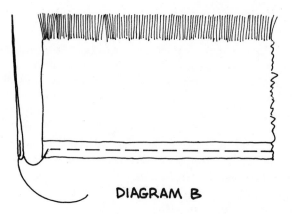

DIAGRAM B

FLOWER ASSEMBLY AND STEM

1. Take the piece of #20 stem wire, bend a hook at one end, and put the hook through the hole in the inner petal, as shown in Diagram C. Twist the hook around the stem to secure.

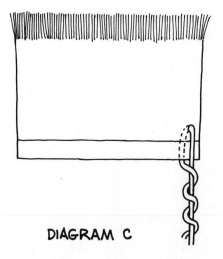

DIAGRAM C

2. With a toothpick, spread a little tacky glue along the inner petal selvedge; roll up the petal tightly around the hook. Secure with a tiny bit of floral tape. (Diagram D.)
3. Take your outer petal and pull the thread to shirr it to fit around the inner petal. Tack in place and cut off the thread.

74

4. Push the calyx up the stem wire close under the petals. Attach to the stem with floral tape.

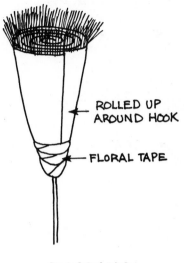

ROLLED UP
AROUND HOOK

FLORAL TAPE

DIAGRAM D

5. Continue taping the top ½ inch of the stem, building it up as shown by the shaded area in Diagram E. Continue taping 2 inches down the stem.

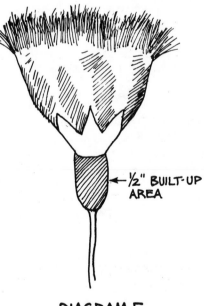

← ½" BUILT-UP AREA

DIAGRAM E

6. Attach the first leaf to the stem, allowing 1 inch of its stem to show. Continue taping another 2 inches down the stem.

7. Attach the second leaf to the stem opposite the first leaf, again letting 1 inch of the leaf stem show. Continue taping another inch down the stem.

8. Attach the third leaf to the stem on the same side as the first leaf. (Add the bud stem at the same time, if you make it.) Continue taping down the stem to the end. Cut off tape.

BUD AND STEM (OPTIONAL)

1. Take the 2-inch piece of trim and make the hole, as shown in Diagram A.

2. Using the piece of #20 stem wire, follow Steps 1 and 2 for Flower Assembly and Stem (above). (Diagrams C, D.)

3. Secure the bud to the stem with floral tape, then build up the stem slightly just under the bud with the tape. Continue taping down to the bottom of the stem. Cut off tape.

4. Attach to the flower stem, taping it in along with the third leaf.

THE CREATIVE TOUCH

Spray-paint a wicker basket white, fill up with a bunch of our carnations, and hang on the door of a powder room or nursery. Tiny dried star flowers and baby's breath make excellent fillers; spray-paint the baby's breath white, too, so it will look pristine.

Chrysanthemum

This marvelous flower consists of twisted ribbon forming loopy petals, all pinned to a styrofoam ball. The stem is glued into the bottom along with a green felt calyx, and it's finished by taping, adding 3 leaves.

MATERIALS FOR 1 FLOWER AND 3 LEAVES

PETAL ASSEMBLY

1-inch-diameter styrofoam ball
108 straight pins, ½ inch long
5 yards corsage ribbon, ½ inch wide, in desired color, cut as follows:
  1 piece, 1 inch long
  4 pieces, each 1¾ inches long
  16 pieces, each 2¾ inches long
  16 pieces, each 3¼ inches long
  8 pieces, each 3¾ inches long
  8 pieces, each 4¾ inches long

FLOWER ASSEMBLY AND STEM

18-inch piece #18 stem wire
white resin glue
½-inch-diameter circle of green felt
green floral tape
3 craft leaves (chrysanthemum type)

Also: scissors; wire cutters

PETAL ASSEMBLY

1. Pin the 1-inch piece of ribbon to the styrofoam ball, as shown in Diagram A. This is the flower center.

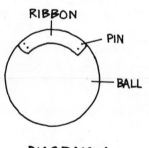

DIAGRAM A

2. Twist a piece of the 1¾-inch ribbon in the middle so the right side shows on one half and the wrong side shows on the other. (Diagram B.) Bring the short ends together to form the petal. (Diagram C.)

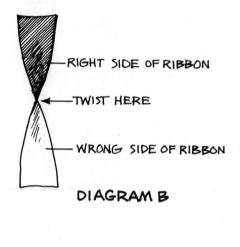

DIAGRAM B

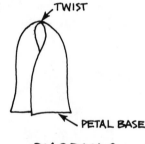

DIAGRAM C

3. Pin petal to styrofoam ball, right side out, near the edge of the flower center. Place as shown in Diagram D, with the twist up and the pins on the outside.

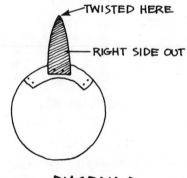

DIAGRAM D

4. Repeat Steps 2 and 3 with the other 1¾-inch ribbon pieces, placing them to form a circle, as shown in Diagram E, with petals slightly overlapping.

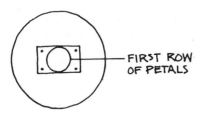

DIAGRAM E

5. Repeat Steps 2, 3 and 4 with the rest of the ribbon, forming petal circles close under each other, the successive circles pinned on in the following order:

8 petals of the 2¾-inch ribbon
8 petals of the 2¾-inch ribbon
8 petals of the 3¼-inch ribbon
8 petals of the 3¼-inch ribbon
4 petals of the 3¾-inch ribbon
4 petals of the 3¾-inch ribbon
4 petals of the 4¾-inch ribbon
4 petals of the 4¾-inch ribbon

Most of the ball will be covered with the petals, but be sure to leave a small empty space exactly at the center bottom.

FLOWER ASSEMBLY AND STEM

1. Dip one end of the #18 stem wire into the glue and insert it straight up into the center bottom of the ball.

2. Take the green felt calyx and, with the tip of your scissors, make a tiny hole in the exact center. Put the stem wire down into the hole and push the calyx up the stem. Put a small bit of glue inside the calyx, then push it up snug against the petals.

3. Attach the calyx to the stem with floral tape and continue taping 4 inches down the stem.

4. Attach 2 leaves to the stem with the tape, placing them opposite each other. Continue taping another inch down the stem.

5. Attach the third leaf to the stem. Continue taping down to the end of the stem. Cut off tape.

THE CREATIVE TOUCH

A single chrysanthemum makes a handsome corsage for a lifetime of football games. Simply shorten the stem, add a ribbon bow in a complementary color, and pin to your coat or suit with a couple of corsage pins!

Denim Flower

This is made just like the Gingham Flower (page 46)—petals are pieces of wire bent to petal shape, glued down to denim ribbon, and cut out. Petals are assembled around a stamen cluster taped to the stem, and finished by taping down.

MATERIALS FOR 1 FLOWER

PETALS

¾ yard denim ribbon, or denim variation ribbon, 2 inches wide
white resin glue or clear craft cement
5 pieces #28 white-covered wire, each 7 inches long
5 pieces #28 white-covered wire, each 9 inches long

FLOWER ASSEMBLY AND STEM

cluster of single craft stamens in desired color
4-inch piece #20 stem wire
green floral tape
¾ yard #28 dark blue-covered wire

Also: wire cutters; toothpicks (to apply glue), wax paper; découpage or manicure scissors

PETALS

1. Bend each of the five 7-inch lengths of #28 covered wire to the small petal shape (Pattern 1). Place the middle of your wire at the top of the pattern, shape the wire down on both sides, and twist them together at the bottom. Do not cut off wire—it is your petal stem.

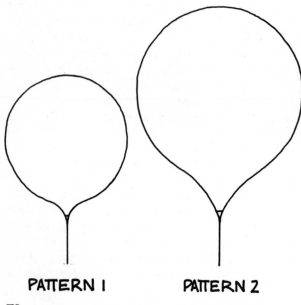

PATTERN 1   **PATTERN 2**

2. Spread out the denim ribbon, wrong side up, on a flat surface. Coat each of your petal shapes with glue (do not coat the stems), and place them sideways on the ribbon, leaving a little space between them (to make it easier when cutting out later). (Diagram A.) Put a piece of wax paper over them and weight with a book until dry.

3. Repeat Steps 1 and 2, using the five 9-inch lengths of #28 covered wire bent to the large petal shape (Pattern 2).

4. When all are dry, use découpage scissors to cut each petal out of the ribbon and trim off, following closely around the edges of the glued wire.

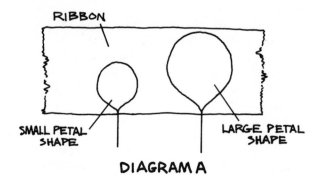

DIAGRAM A

FLOWER ASSEMBLY AND STEM

1. Attach the stamen cluster to one end of the #20 stem wire, using floral tape. Cut off the tape.

2. Using the #28 covered wire, attach the 5 small petals around the stamen cluster, one at a time, overlapping them slightly.

3. Attach the 5 large petals just beneath and around the small petals in the same way, placing them one at a time and with petal tips staggered. Cut off the #28 wire.

4. With the floral tape, start taping at the base of the petals, covering the binding wire, and continue taping down the stem wire to the end. Cut off tape.

5. Shape the petals by cupping.

THE CREATIVE TOUCH

Here is a fabulous Christmas decoration when you have teen-agers living at home: Make lots of denim flowers and attach them to a small artificial tree with metal hair clips painted in a matching or contrasting color. We've added checkered bows and small doll ornaments to our tree, but we also like to see animal cookie cutters painted in bright colors tied to the tree along with the flowers.

Fantasy Flower

Like the Denim Flower just preceding, this is made by bending wire to form petals, gluing them to ribbon, and cutting them out. The petals are assembled around a cluster of pearl stamens taped to a stem wire, and finished by taping. What makes these flowers different, besides the petal shapes, is the mélange of colors and patterns you'll make them in, for a truly fantastic effect.

MATERIALS FOR 1 FLOWER

PETALS

½ yard ribbon, 2½ inches wide, in desired color and pattern
5 pieces #28 covered wire in color compatible with ribbon, each 5 inches long
5 pieces same #28 covered wire, each 6 inches long
white resin glue or clear craft cement

FLOWER ASSEMBLY AND STEM

cluster of pearl stamens in desired color
8-inch piece #20 stem wire
green floral tape
½ yard #28 covered wire, same color as above

Also: wire cutters; toothpicks (to apply glue), wax paper; découpage or manicure scissors

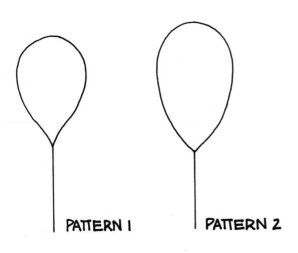

PATTERN 1   **PATTERN 2**

PETALS

1. Bend each of the five 5-inch lengths of #28 covered wire to the shape of Pattern 1. These are your small petal shapes. Place the middle of the wire at the top of the pattern, shape the wire down on both sides, and twist the ends together at the bottom. Do not cut off the wire—it's your petal stem.

2. Spread the ribbon on a flat surface, wrong side up. One at a time, coat each of the small petal shapes with glue (do not coat the stems), then place them on the ribbon. (Diagram A.) Place a piece of wax paper over them and weight with a book until dry.

3. Repeat Steps 1 and 2, using the five 6-inch lengths of #28 covered wire bent to the shape of Pattern 2. These are your large petal shapes.

4. When dry, use découpage scissors to cut each petal out of the ribbon; trim it off, following closely around the shape of the glued wire.

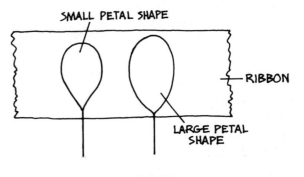

SMALL PETAL SHAPE

RIBBON

LARGE PETAL SHAPE

DIAGRAM A

FLOWER ASSEMBLY AND STEM

1. Attach the stamen cluster to one end of the #20 stem wire, using floral tape. Cut off tape.

2. Attach the 5 small petals around the stamen cluster, using their own hanging tails of covered wire and the additional #28 covered wire. Attach them one at a time, right side in toward the stamens, overlapping them slightly. Cut off excess covered wire.

3. Repeat Step 2 with the 5 large petals, placing them just under the small petals, making sure to stagger the petal tips. Cut off excess covered wire.

4. Begin again with the floral tape, starting at the top of the stem just under the petals, taping over the covered wires; continue taping down to the end of the stem. Cut off tape.

5. Shape the petals by cupping.

THE CREATIVE TOUCH

Decorate a plastic flowerpot with scraps of fabric, ribbon and eyelet trim; paint everything with several coats of glue to stiffen. Trim the top of the pot with velvet ribbon, then fill it with fantasy flowers, dried baby's breath and little velvet bows. What an adorable accent for a powder room or a vanity tabletop!

Poinsettia

This opulent Christmas flower is easily made with red velvet ribbon and red-covered wire bent to petal shapes, glued, and cut out. Assembled around a pep attached to a stem wire, it is finished by taping, adding 2 velvet ribbon leaves (made just like the petals).

MATERIALS FOR 1 FLOWER AND 2 LEAVES

PETALS

1 yard satin-backed red velvet corsage ribbon, 1½ inches wide
5 pieces #28 red-covered wire, each 8 inches long
7 pieces #28 red-covered wire, each 9 inches long
white resin glue

LEAVES

½ yard satin-backed green velvet corsage ribbon, 1½ inches wide
2 pieces #28 green-covered wire, each 10 inches long
white resin glue

FLOWER ASSEMBLY AND STEM

pep (poinsettia type)
6-inch piece #18 stem wire
green floral tape

Also: wire cutters; toothpicks (to apply glue); découpage or manicure scissors

PETALS

1. Bend the five 8-inch lengths of red-covered wire to the shape of Pattern 1. These are your small petal shapes. Place the middle of the wire at the top of the pattern, shape the wire down on both sides, and twist them together at the bottom. Do not cut off the wire—it's your petal stem.
2. Repeat Step 1, using the seven 9-inch lengths of red-covered wire bent to the shape of Pattern 2. These are your large petal shapes.
3. Spread the red velvet ribbon on a flat surface, satin side up. One at a time, coat each of the petal shapes with glue (do not coat the stems), then place them on the red velvet ribbon. Let dry.
4. When dry, use découpage scissors to cut each petal out of the ribbon; trim it off, following closely around the shape of the glued wire.

LEAVES

1. Repeat Step 1 for petals, using the two 10-inch pieces of green-covered wire bent to the shape of Pattern 3.
2. Repeat Steps 3 and 4 for petals, using the green velvet ribbon and the 2 pieces of green-covered wire.

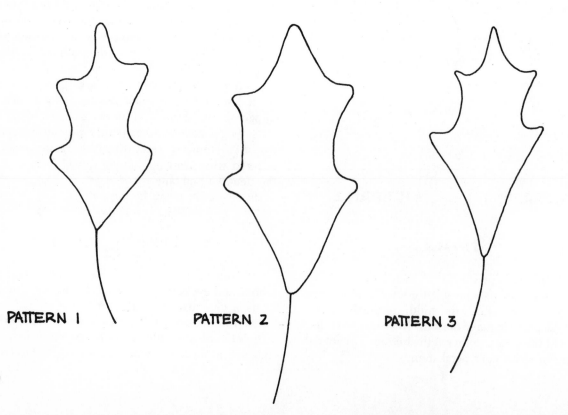

PATTERN 1   PATTERN 2   PATTERN 3

FLOWER ASSEMBLY AND STEM

1. Attach the pep to one end of the #18 stem wire, using floral tape. Cut off tape.

2. Attach the 5 small petals around the pep, using their own hanging tails of red-covered wire. Attach them one at a time, velvet side in, fanning them out as you proceed. Cut off excess red wire.

3. Repeat Step 2 with the 7 large petals, placing them just under the small petals, making sure to stagger the petal tips.

4. Start again with the floral tape at the top of the stem just under the petals, covering the red wires, then tape 1½ inches down the stem wire.

5. Attach 1 leaf to the stem with the floral tape. Continue taping another inch down the stem.

6. Attach the second leaf to the stem opposite the first leaf. Continue taping down to the end of the stem. Cut off tape.

7. Shape the petals by cupping slightly.

THE CREATIVE TOUCH

Most of the time we make these rich-looking flowers to trim Christmas packages for special people, but on more than one occasion we have tucked a few handmade poinsettias into our live poinsettia plant after its own blooms have faded or died.

Rickrack Flower

Another easy one. Petals consist of 2 shades of rickrack tightly gathered and tacked into a circle. They are then assembled around a stamen cluster wired to a stem wire, the flower finished by taping down the stem.

MATERIALS FOR 1 FLOWER

PETAL UNIT

12-inch piece rickrack in desired color
12-inch piece rickrack in contrasting color
sewing thread

FLOWER ASSEMBLY AND STEM

cluster of craft stamens in desired color
7-inch piece #18 stem wire
small piece #28 covered wire
green floral tape

Also: scissors, sewing needle; wire cutters

PETAL UNIT

1. Place your 2 pieces of rickrack together with points matching. With needle and thread, sew them together through the points along one edge, as shown in Diagram A.
2. Pull the thread tightly, gathering the petal unit into a small circle. Tack the two ends together, knotting the thread to secure. (Diagram B.)

FLOWER ASSEMBLY AND STEM

1. Attach the stamen cluster to one end of the piece of #18 stem wire, using a small piece of #28 covered wire. Cut off excess covered wire.
2. Tape over the covered wire with floral tape. Cut off tape.
3. Put the bottom of the stem wire down through the center of the petal unit, drawing it down until the petal sits firmly around the stamen cluster.
4. Start again with the floral tape, just under the petal unit, building up the top ¼ inch of the stem, as shown by the shaded area in Diagram C. Tape down the stem to the end. Cut off tape.

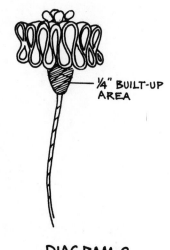

¼" BUILT-UP AREA

DIAGRAM C

THE CREATIVE TOUCH

We like to combine several rickrack posies with dried statice that has been spray-painted in lavender. A charming kitchen arrangement is composed of green rickrack flowers and small artificial potatoes in a coffee mug.

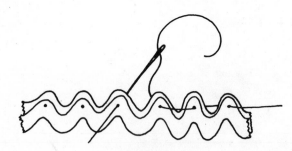

DIAGRAM A

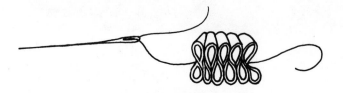

DIAGRAM B

FIVE

Flowers from Paper

Flowers made from paper are attractive, inexpensive, and fun to create. Few other materials come in such a wide variety of colors, textures and patterns, and few decorations can provide so much pizzazz for the amount of money invested.

The projects in this chapter have been designed especially for the more casual rooms in your home, such as a teen-ager's bedroom, the family room, the kitchen and bath, or any niche where a bright spot of color is desired.

Paper flowers are also an exceptionally suitable decoration for benefit fashion shows, bridge tournaments and bazaars. In fact, after the flowers have served their decorative purpose, but before the event has ended, they can be put up for sale and help add dollars to the profits.

Paper carnation, page 85

Paper daisy, page 87

Carnation

It's hard to believe that this elegant carnation is made of ordinary facial tissues and crepe paper! The many-layered flower is made of 2 double tissues, folded, edges pinked, folded again, then gathered and bound around with wire. It's taped to a stem wire, then finished by taping, adding a crepe-paper calyx and crepe-paper leaves.

MATERIALS FOR 1 FLOWER AND 4 LEAVES

PETAL UNITS

2 facial tissues, each 2-ply, in desired color
#28 spool wire

LEAVES

1 sheet green duplex crepe paper

FLOWER ASSEMBLY AND STEM

10-inch piece #18 stem wire
green floral tape
small piece green duplex crepe paper (above)
white resin glue
clear acrylic sealer

Also: pinking shears; wire cutters; pencil, tissue paper, scissors

PETAL UNITS

1. Unfold the 2 facial tissues and place them one on top of the other. Fold in half, as shown by the dotted line in Diagram A.
2. With the pinking shears, cut across both long edges, as shown in Diagram B.

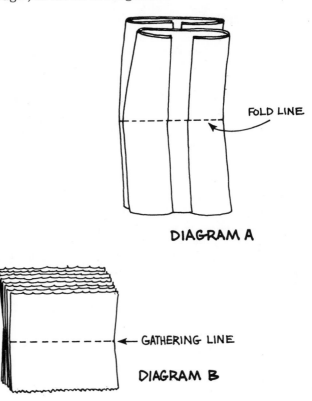

FOLD LINE

DIAGRAM A

GATHERING LINE

DIAGRAM B

3. With the pinked pieces still flat on your work surface, use your thumbs and forefingers to gather them across the middle, as shown by the dotted line in Diagram B. Secure by wrapping around the middle with #28 spool wire (Diagram C), but don't cut off the wire.
4. Bring the 2 gathered sides together by pinching tightly around the wire-wrapped part (Diagram D). Pick up the #28 spool wire and wrap tightly around the outside of the base to secure. Cut off the spool wire very close.

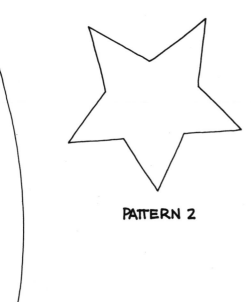

PATTERN 2

PATTERN 1

DIAGRAM C

LEAVES

1. Make tissue paper Pattern 1, tracing from book pattern. Cut 4 leaves out of green crepe paper from Pattern 1.

2. Shape the leaves by curling.

FLOWER ASSEMBLY AND STEM

1. Attach the base of the flower to one end of the #18 stem wire, using floral tape. Cut off tape.

2. Make tissue paper Pattern 2, tracing from book pattern. Cut 1 calyx out of the green crepe paper from Pattern 2.

3. With the tip of your scissors, make a tiny hole in the exact center of the calyx. Put the bottom end of the stem wire down through the hole in the calyx and push the calyx up the stem right under the flower base, securing with a dot of glue.

4. Start again with the floral tape, at the base of the calyx, and tape down the stem for 3 inches.

5. Attach a leaf to the stem with the tape. Continue taping another ¾ inch down the stem.

6. Attach another leaf to the stem opposite the first leaf. Continue taping another ¾ inch down the stem.

7. Attach the other 2 leaves to the stem in the same way, alternating sides, then finish taping down to the bottom of the stem. Cut off tape.

8. Fluff out the flower and spray with clear acrylic sealer.

THE CREATIVE TOUCH

A single carnation makes a snappy boutonniere or a trimming for a gift package. Or consider decorating the tables of a large luncheon with bouquets of carnations—and for containers, you can use plastic margarine tubs or those cheap florist's bowls you can't bear to throw away. Camouflage the containers by filling them with Oasis and clumps of real evergreen, then stick in your carnations—in this case, you can omit the crepe-paper leaves.

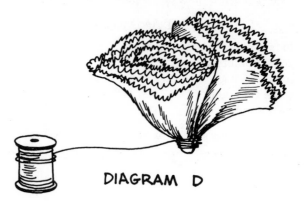

DIAGRAM D

Daisy

A crepe-paper oblong is folded and petal tips cut out, then it's gathered and wired, folded again—and there's a double ring of daisy petals, real as can be. The yellow center (also of crepe paper, wrapped around a tiny cotton ball) is wired to the stem, the petals assembled around it. The stem is finished by taping, adding a sprig of craft leaves.

MATERIALS FOR 1 FLOWER AND 1 SPRIG OF LEAVES

PETAL UNIT

1 sheet white duplex crepe paper
#28 spool wire

FLOWER CENTER

1 sheet yellow duplex crepe paper
absorbent cotton cosmetics ball
#28 spool wire

FLOWER ASSEMBLY AND STEM

10-inch piece #18 stem wire
#28 spool wire
green floral tape
1 sprig craft leaves (daisy type)

Also: ruler, pencil, scissors; wire cutters, compass

PETAL UNIT

1. With a pencil and ruler, draw a 3 × 6½-inch oblong directly onto the white crepe paper. With the scissors, cut out along the ruled lines. This is your petal unit.
2. Fold the petal unit in half along the dotted line shown in Diagram A.
3. Fold in half again along the dotted line shown in Diagram B.
4. Fold in half again along the dotted line shown in Diagram C.

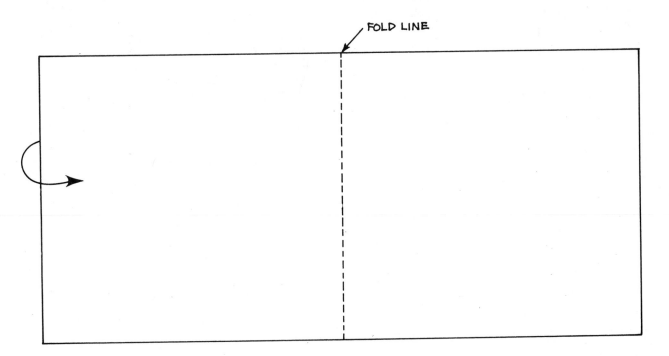

FOLD LINE

DIAGRAM A

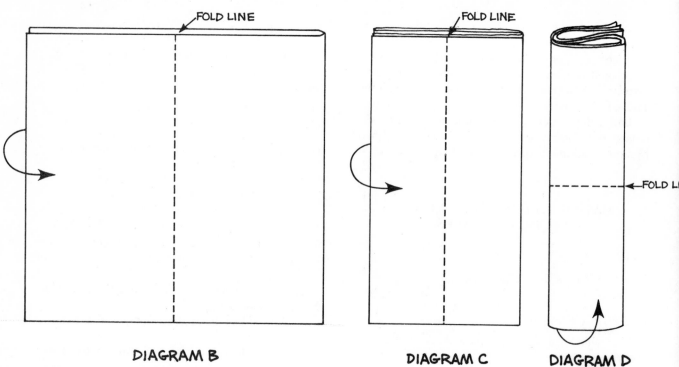

FOLD LINE

DIAGRAM B

FOLD LINE

DIAGRAM C

FOLD L|

DIAGRAM D

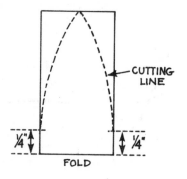

CUTTING
LINE

¼   ¼"

FOLD

DIAGRAM E

5. Finally, fold in half in the other direction, along the dotted line shown in Diagram D.

6. Press down flat, then, using your scissors, cut through all layers: starting ¼ inch above the fold on each side, cut nice curves meeting at the center top, as shown by the dotted line in Diagram E.

7. Unfold after cutting and spread out flat. You'll have 8 petals above and 8 below. Use your thumbs and forefingers to gather the piece together across the middle, as shown by the dotted line in Diagram F. Pinch tightly, making sure end petals meet, then

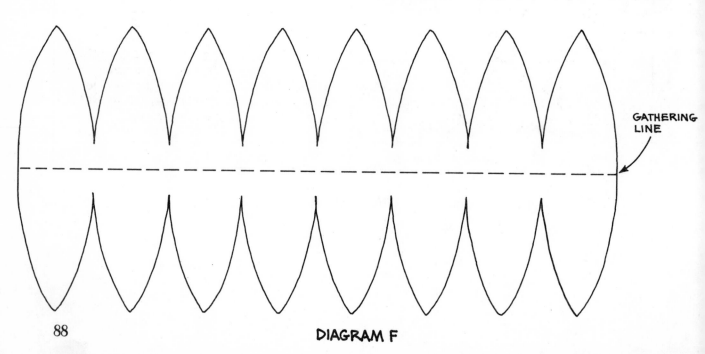

GATHERING
LINE

DIAGRAM F

secure by wrapping around the middle with #28 spool wire, as shown in Diagram G. Cut off the wire very close.

8. Turn the lower petals up around the top ones, making a double row of petals, as shown in Diagram H.

9. Shape the petals by cupping.

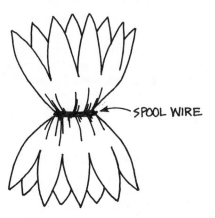

DIAGRAM G

DIAGRAM H

FLOWER CENTER

1. With a compass, draw a circle 2 inches in diameter directly onto the yellow crepe paper. Using your scissors, cut out around the penciled line.

2. Cover the absorbent cotton ball smoothly with the yellow crepe-paper circle, drawing the paper together underneath. (Diagram I.) Secure it tightly with a bit of #28 spool wire, but do not cut the wire off the spool. Trim off excess crepe paper, leaving ¼ inch below the wire.

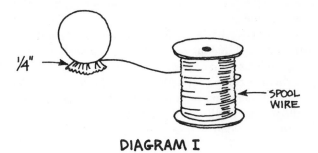

DIAGRAM I

FLOWER ASSEMBLY AND STEM

1. Push one end of the #18 stem wire up into the bottom of the flower center. Now use the #28 spool wire to secure the bottom of the flower center to the stem wire, wrapping it around tightly. Cut off the spool wire very close.

2. Put the bottom end of the stem wire down through the center of the petal unit until the flower center rests snug against the petals.

3. Attach the underside of the flower to the stem wire using floral tape, then continue taping down the stem for 4 or 5 inches.

4. Attach the sprig of leaves to the stem with tape, then finish taping down to the bottom of the stem. Cut off tape.

THE CREATIVE TOUCH

One of us had an old, wooden, bucket-shaped handbag no longer in use, so we painted it white, glued on daisy prints from a crafts store, sealed the prints with two coats of Mod Podge, then filled the bucket with a dozen of our daisies.

Three-Dimensional Poppy Picture

A lovely three-dimensional print is created by cutting out duplicate pieces of a picture, shaping and rounding the cutouts, then mounting them one over the other on a master canvas. To finish, spray the completed 3-D picture with acrylic sealer, then mat and frame.

This is the basic technique for *papier tôle* or three-dimensional découpage, and, although we have used a particular print of poppies for this project, the same technique can be applied to prints of other flowers in other dimensions, or to prints of other subject matter altogether. The Bernard prints used in this project are available in crafts stores.

MATERIALS FOR ONE 3-DIMENSIONAL CANVAS PRINT

four 18 × 22-inch #FL951 Bernard prints
18 × 22-inch canvas board
spray adhesive
Derwent oil pencil in brown
Dow Chemical silicone adhesive
picture mat in desired material and color (optional)
white resin glue (optional)
spray acrylic sealer in matte finish
picture frame

Also: brayer; découpage scissors or X-acto professional swivel knife or X-acto No. 1 knife; burnisher; toothpicks, wax paper or aluminum foil (for applying spray adhesive); tweezers

FIRST STEPS

1. Apply the spray adhesive to the front of the canvas board and to the back of one of the prints. When the sprayed surfaces feel tacky to the touch, mount the print onto the canvas board and use a brayer to eliminate all bubbles, rolling it out from the center to the edges of the print.

2. Place a second print on a work surface (a board is best for this) and, using the X-acto knife, cut away the flowers and the basket from the background. (Diagram A.) The most effective way to use the knife is as follows: Cut the print from left to right, holding the knife at a 45° angle to make a clean, close cut, and to provide a beveled edge. Apply very little pressure; just guide the knife along and let it do the work instead of your arm or hand. The swivel knife is preferred for this project because its ball-bearing

action makes the cutting quicker and easier and gives a good edge.

3. Holding the cutout print in the palm of your hand, give parts of it a little bit of a rounded, raised shape by pressing on the wrong side with a burnisher.

4. Dip the tip of the oil pencil into water and touch up any white edges that may show on the cutout pieces. The pencil application will soften the edges to give the picture additional dimension.

5. Study the remaining 2 prints very carefully before you begin to cut; then cut them out according to Diagrams B and C, following the cutting directions in Step 2. Discard anything not shown in the diagrams and keep the cutouts of each print separate, except put the black calyx pieces from the "B" cutouts with the "C" cutouts.

6. Using the burnisher and the palm of your hand, shape each cutout piece as closely to its actual shape as possible. Leaves should be placed in the palm of your hand facing up and pressed with the burnisher down the middle. Place concave petals in the palm right side up and press with the burnisher; place convex petals in the palm facing down and press likewise. Round the edges of the petals with the burnisher.

7. Color the edges of all the cutout pieces with the oil pencil, as described in Step 4.

PRINT ASSEMBLY

1. Apply silicone adhesive to the flowers, buds, leaves and basket edges of the print glued to the canvas board, taking care, each time you squeeze the silicone adhesive out of the tube, to pull the tube away abruptly to form a peak of adhesive like the peak of a beaten egg white. When all the adhesive has been applied, gently place the cutout print from Diagram A on top of the canvas board print so the outlines of the two line up perfectly; *do not press down* on the top print in order to achieve a raised effect.

2. Apply silicone adhesive to the backs of the cutout pieces from Diagram B (except the black calyxes), starting with the cutouts at the top of the picture and working down to those at the bottom. For the larger cutouts, pull the tube up abruptly when squeezing on the adhesive so as to form a peak like the peak of a beaten egg white. For the smaller cutouts, squeeze a little adhesive onto some wax paper or aluminum foil, then apply to the cutout with a toothpick, but still use the motion of pulling up

abruptly. *Important:* Work on the cutouts one at a time, proceeding to take each cutout through Step 3 before applying adhesive to the next cutout.

3. Using tweezers to pick up and place the cutout pieces, gently place each one on the spot to which it corresponds on the raised cutout prints from Diagram A, now mounted on the canvas board, making sure the outlines are in perfect alignment. *Do not press down* on the cutout pieces in order to achieve a raised effect. Remove any excess adhesive with a toothpick. Let dry completely.

If a cutout piece becomes flattened by accident while still wet, simply lift it up and clean it off, then reshape and reapply it as before. If a cutout dries before you notice it has been flattened, cut it away with the X-acto knife, then reshape and reapply it.

4. Repeat Steps 2 and 3 for the cutout pieces from Diagram C, along with the black calyx pieces, which are applied last.

5. Glue a mat to the front edges of the canvas board (optional).

6. Lightly spray the completed picture with acrylic sealer.

7. Frame the picture yourself or have it framed.

THE CREATIVE TOUCH

We framed our poppies in a lovely gold-leaf frame, the mat of which was covered with red velvet to match the flowers. This kind of picture sells in galleries for several hundred dollars, so do not compromise on the quality of the frame.

DIAGRAM A

DIAGRAM B

DIAGRAM C

91

Papier-Mâché Posies

Three big bright flowers are cut out of papier-mâché from a cardboard pattern, then covered front and back with gift wrap paper and trimmed with acrylic paint. The flower centers are made of painted papier-mâché half-circles. The finished flowers and 5 craft leaves are attached to a soldered stem-wire base, which is centered and secured in a tin filled with plaster of Paris. The stems are finished off with green velvet ribbon; the tin base with paper and velvet ribbon trim.

MATERIALS FOR 3 FLOWERS AND 5 LEAVES

STEMS

40-inch piece #16 stem wire or heavy wire coat hangers

PETAL UNITS

1-pound bag instant papier-mâché
gift wrap paper in desired pattern
acrylic paint in color to coordinate with gift wrap paper
white resin glue

FLOWER CENTERS

some of the papier-mâché from above
acrylic paint (see above)

FLOWER ASSEMBLY AND STEM

liquid solder
floral tape
1-pound bag plaster of Paris
30-ounce tin can
white resin glue
5 large craft leaves (rose type)
2 yards green velvet ribbon, ¼ inch wide

FLOWERPOT ASSEMBLY

gift wrap paper in desired pattern (see above)
white resin glue
1 yard velvet ribbon, ¼ inch wide, in desired color
dried sheet moss (optional)

Also: wire cutters; large bowl; tissue paper, cardboard, scissors; wax paper, rolling pin; sharp knife; small artist's paintbrush

PATTERN 1

STEMS

Cut the #16 stem wire into one 18-inch piece, one 9-inch piece, one 8-inch piece, and two 2½-inch pieces. Set aside. The 3 longer pieces will be your flower stems; the 2 smaller pieces will be for 2 of the 5 leaves.

PETAL UNITS

1. Mix the papier-mâché according to package directions. Knead the mixture with your hands until it has the consistency of putty, adding a few drops of water if the mixture becomes too dry. Put the mixture into the refrigerator until ready to use. (The 1-pound bag will yield more papier-mâché than you need for this project, but it will keep in the refrigerator for several days.)

2. Make a tissue paper pattern, tracing from book Pattern 1. Cut 1 petal unit out of cardboard from the tissue pattern. The cardboard will be your petal unit pattern.

3. Remove half of the papier-mâché from the refrigerator, place it between 2 sheets of wax paper, and roll it out with a rolling pin to a thickness of ¼ inch. Remove the top sheet of wax paper.

4. Place the cardboard pattern on the papier-mâché and cut around it with a sharp knife; repeat twice for a total of 3 petal units.

5. As the papier-mâché begins to set, curl the petals inward toward each other with your fingers, or leave the petal units flat if you prefer.

6. Stick one end of the 3 longer pieces of the #16 stem wire about 2 inches into each petal unit, as shown in Diagram A, then remove the wires to let the

holes dry. Set aside the petal units for several days, until they are completely dry.

7. Using the cardboard pattern for the petal units, cut 6 petal units out of the gift wrap paper and glue them onto the front and back of each papier-mâché petal unit.

8. Using the small artist's paintbrush, touch up the sides of the petal units with acrylic paint. Set aside to dry.

FLOWER CENTERS

1. For the flower centers, roll up some of the papier-mâché mixture into 2 balls, each the size of a ping-pong ball (about 1¼ inches in diameter). Slice the balls in half with a sharp knife. Set aside 3 of the halves for several days, until completely dry. Discard the fourth half, or save for another flower.

2. When dry, paint the flower centers with the acrylic paint. Set aside to dry.

FLOWER ASSEMBLY AND STEM

1. Put a dab of liquid solder on one end of the 8- and 9-inch pieces of #16 stem wire and attach to one end of the 18-inch piece to make the stem unit. (Diagram B.) Attach the two 2½-inch pieces of stem wire to the stem unit with liquid solder; place as desired. Wrap floral tape around the soldered joints until the solder has hardened, then remove the tape.

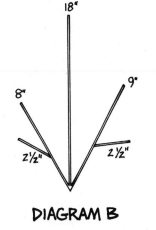

DIAGRAM B

2. Following directions on the package, mix enough plaster of Paris to fill the tin can to within ½ inch of the top, then insert about 2 inches of the stem unit base into the plaster of Paris and hold it there until the plaster hardens.

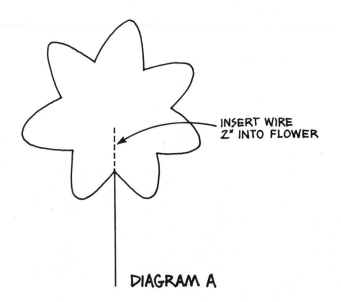

INSERT WIRE 2" INTO FLOWER

DIAGRAM A

3. Glue the painted flower centers to the exact centers of the petal units.

4. Put a small amount of glue on the ends of the 3 long stems and push into the holes of the finished flower petal units.

5. With floral tape, tape 2 of the craft leaves to the ends of the short 2½-inch stems. Tape the 3 remaining leaves to the 3 long flower stems where desired.

6. Wrap the green velvet ribbon around all the stems, securing at the top and bottom of each stem with glue.

FLOWERPOT ASSEMBLY

1. Cut a piece of the gift wrap paper to fit around the tin can and glue in place.

2. Glue the velvet ribbon in desired color around the top and bottom of the can.

3. If you wish, cut a circle out of dried sheet moss the same diameter as the top of the tin can; make a

slash in the moss as indicated by the dotted line in Diagram C. Fit the moss around the base of the stem unit, covering the top of the can.

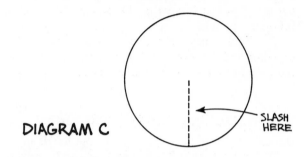

DIAGRAM C — SLASH HERE

THE CREATIVE TOUCH

These sturdy and cheerful posies are perfect for brightening up a kitchen-dining area, or any room that receives a lot of wear and tear. For a variation, try covering them with leftover fabric, or just paint the flowers with a bright and imaginative design!

Papier-mâché posies make an excellent school project as well.

Giant Rose

A big charming flower in a pot—very easy to make. Petal units are scalloped lengths of crepe paper wound around a stem wire. The stem is strengthened by taping to a wooden dowel, adding in 3 (wired) crepe-paper leaves. The dowel-stem is inserted into a flowerpot weighted with rocks or gravel—and covered with dried sheet moss to finish.

MATERIALS FOR 1 FLOWER AND 3 LEAVES

PETAL UNITS

1 package duplex crepe paper in desired color

LEAVES

1 sheet green duplex crepe paper
3 pieces #20 stem wire, each 16 inches long
white resin glue

FLOWER ASSEMBLY AND STEM

24-inch piece #16 stem wire
20-inch piece #28 green-covered wire
green floral tape

GIANT ROSE AND FLOWERPOT ASSEMBLY

18-inch piece ⅜-inch dowel
floral tape
terra-cotta flowerpot
rocks or gravel
dried sheet moss

Also: ruler, pencil, tissue paper, scissors; wire cutters; toothpicks, wax paper or aluminum foil (for gluing)

PETAL UNITS

1. Before opening the folded package of crepe paper, cut 4 inches off one end. Before unfolding the 4-inch section, cut a petal shape out of it, as indicated by the dotted line in Diagram A.

2. Cut the rest of the crepe-paper package in half to make two 8-inch sections, and cut petal shapes out of these sections in the same way as directed in Step 1 (Diagram B).

LEAVES

1. Make tissue paper Pattern 1, tracing from book pattern. Cut 6 leaves out of the green crepe paper, following Pattern 1.

2. Using white resin glue, wire 2 of the leaves together with 1 piece of #20 stem wire. Repeat with the remaining 4 leaves to make 3 finished leaves.

FLOWER ASSEMBLY AND STEM

1. Bend one end of the #16 stem wire into a large hook.

2. Unfold the 4-inch section of crepe paper. Roll up the paper tightly around the hook in the #16 stem wire so that the hook is concealed. As you are rolling, gather the paper tightly along the long bottom edge. Secure the petals at the base with the #28 covered wire.

3. Repeat Step 2 with each 8-inch section of crepe paper, making sure to stagger the placement of the petals as the petal rows are wrapped around and just under one another. Secure the petals to the stem wire at their base with the #28 covered wire.

4. Cut off any excess wire, and, beginning at the base of the flower, tape down the stem wire with floral tape. Cut off tape at end.

5. Spread the petals and shape them by cupping, curling and fluting.

GIANT ROSE AND FLOWERPOT ASSEMBLY

1. Attach the #16 stem wire to the dowel with floral tape and tape to within 5 or 6 inches of the end of the dowel, taping in the 3 wired leaves as you tape down the dowel. Finish taping to the end of the dowel. Cut off tape.

2. Fill the flowerpot with rocks or gravel and insert the end of the dowel. (The rocks will prevent the heavy rose from toppling over.) Cover the rocks with some dried sheet moss.

3. Decorate the flowerpot, if desired.

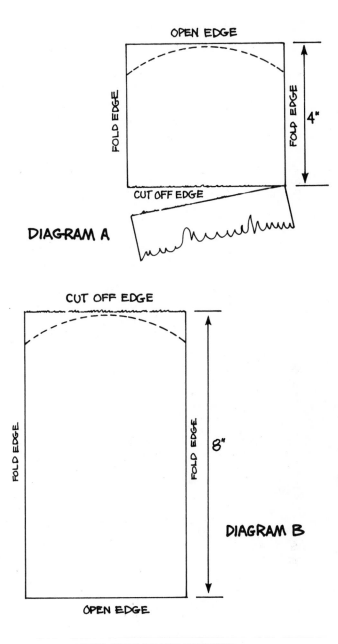

THE CREATIVE TOUCH

This flower is particularly attractive when combined with cattails and arranged in a duck decoy container for a family room, den or office.

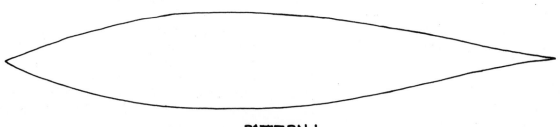

**PATTERN 1
SHOWN HALF SIZE**

SIX

Flowers from Nature

Flowers that are made with Mother Nature's materials are not only practically free, they are also lovely mementos of a summer vacation at the seashore or a walk in the autumn woods. So whenever you find yourself in a natural setting, don't forget to be a collector of whatever is handy, such as shells, grasses, pine cones, leaves, nuts and berries.

Of course not all of us live in the woods or the country or can visit a beach with any regularity. Happily, all the natural materials used in the projects in this chapter can be purchased either in a grocery store, a crafts store or at a garden center.

Artichoke flower, page 98

Feathery flower, page 99

Mushroom flower, page 100

Pine-cone flower, page 101

Tea rose, page 102

Pompon, page 103

Two seashell flowers,
above and right,
page 106

Miniature seashell bouquet, page 108

Artichoke Flower

Simplest of all. If you can refrain from cooking up this edible, natural "flower," all you need do is insert a long stem wire into the artichoke stem, separate and spread the petals open with cotton batting, then set the fruit aside to dry in an upright container. To finish, the artichoke stem can be trimmed down, then covered with brown floral tape along with the stem wire. Or, if you prefer, use it without the long stem in a centerpiece or wreath arrangement.

MATERIALS FOR 1 FLOWER

green artichoke without any blemishes
10-inch piece #16 stem wire
cotton batting
1-quart glass soft-drink bottle
matte-finish acrylic sealer

Also: sharp knife, scissors, brown floral tape (optional)

FLOWER PREPARATION

1. Insert one end of the #16 stem wire about 2 inches into the center of the artichoke stem. (Diagram A.)

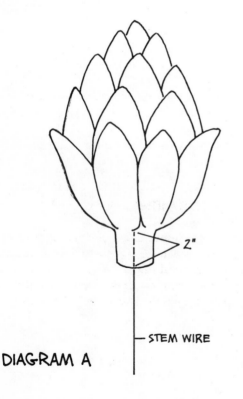

DIAGRAM A

2. Beginning at the base of the artichoke, push back the first layer of petals. Do this for each layer of petals until you reach the tip of the fruit.

3. Starting at the tip of the artichoke, tuck in tiny pieces of cotton batting to keep the petals spread open, until you have covered the entire fruit. Try to tuck the batting in as close as possible to the petal base because the artichoke will stay slightly green wherever there is batting, and you want the final result to be brown.

4. Place the stem wire into the glass bottle so the artichoke is upright, and let the fruit dry for 2 to 3 weeks.

FLOWER ASSEMBLY AND STEM

1. When completely dried and brown, remove from the bottle.

2. With a sharp knife, trim down the sides of the artichoke stem slightly toward the stem wire. Using brown floral tape, begin taping around the trimmed artichoke stem. Continue taping down the stem wire to the end. Cut off tape.

3. If you prefer to use the artichoke in a centerpiece or wreath arrangement, simply shorten the #16 stem wire after Step 1.

BUD (OPTIONAL)

To make an artichoke "bud" omit the cotton batting and push back the petals a little each day until the artichoke has dried.

THE CREATIVE TOUCH

These flowers look simply fabulous when combined with a wreath of hay and dried baby's breath. Or combine with other dried flowers and baby's breath for a table centerpiece.

Feathery Flower

A delicate flower of autumn materials, this is quite easy to assemble. A small seedpod forms the flower center, surrounded by feathery "petals" of pampas grass—all glued into a small pine-cone base that has been wired to a long stem, the stem finished off with brown floral tape.

Before you begin, this is a project that can be fun to collect materials for: pine cones, seedpods or thistleheads from the woods; pampas grass picked by the roadside or found in a marsh. Or, of course, all can be purchased from a store selling dried natural materials.

MATERIALS FOR 1 FLOWER

PETALS

piece of dried pampas grass

FLOWER CENTER

seedpod from sweet gum tree (or ball fringe, dried cloverhead or small thistlehead)

FLOWER ASSEMBLY AND STEM

small pine cone with stem
10-inch piece #18 stem wire
#28 spool wire
brown floral tape
white resin glue or clear craft cement

Also: scissors; small handsaw; wire cutters; toothpicks, tweezers, wax paper or aluminum foil (for gluing)

PETALS

Cut off the feathery ends of the pampas grass into 4-inch lengths and set aside. Discard the stem.

FLOWER ASSEMBLY AND STEM

1. Using a small handsaw, cut off the bottom end of the pine cone as indicated by the dotted line in Diagram A. Discard the top.
2. Wire the stem of the pine cone to one end of the #18 stem wire, using the #28 spool wire.

3. Starting at the base of the pine cone, cover the spool wire with the floral tape. Continue taping down the stem wire to the end. Cut off tape.
4. Using a toothpick, apply glue inside the pine cone and attach the 4-inch pieces of pampas grass, as shown in Diagram B.

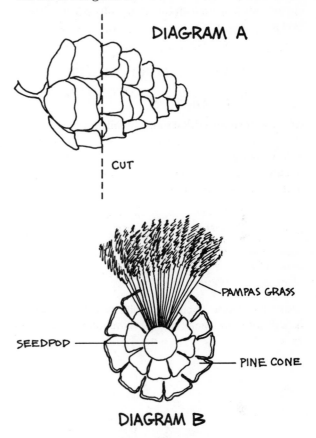

5. Glue the seedpod to the exact center of the pine cone, as shown in Diagram B. Put aside until glued pieces have set.
6. Trim the ends of the pampas grass to 2 inches or to whatever size flower you desire.

THE CREATIVE TOUCH

This flower is especially useful and attractive as a stage decoration at a school function, such as a fashion show or musical revue. We like to decorate the flowerpot by gluing on printed paper napkins and tying a bow around the stem under the flower.

Mushroom Flower

Snappy and simple—a large mushroom with trimmed stem is dried and hardened in silica gel. Before drying, part of a toothpick is inserted through the cap, the toothpick later taped to a length of stem wire and finished with floral tape to form the flower stem. The inside of the mushroom cap is painted black; the unpainted, trimmed mushroom stem is your flower center.

MATERIALS FOR 1 FLOWER

FLOWER PREPARATION

large mushroom without any blemishes
toothpick
white resin glue
silica gel
round fruitcake tin or cookie tin with lid
masking tape

FLOWER ASSEMBLY AND STEM

4-inch piece #20 stem wire or floral pick
green floral tape
black acrylic paint

Also: sharp knife, scissors; small artist's paintbrush (for dusting and painting)

FLOWER PREPARATION

1. With a sharp knife, trim the stem on the mushroom until it is almost level with the cap.
2. Break a toothpick in half, dip the tip into glue, and insert the glued end ½ inch into the mushroom cap up into part of the stem, as shown in Diagram A.
3. Pour a ½-inch layer of silica gel into the fruitcake tin.
4. Place the mushroom, stem side up, on the silica gel. Very slowly pour more silica gel from your hand in a thin stream over the mushroom until it is completely covered.
5. Put the lid on the fruitcake tin and seal it with masking tape. After a couple of days, open up the tin to see if the mushroom has dried out and is hard; if not, reseal the tin and check in another day. (You can dry several mushrooms in the tin at the same time as long as the mushrooms don't touch one another.)
6. Blow the excess silica gel off the mushroom. Then, with the small artist's paintbrush, go over the mushroom to remove every trace of silica gel.

FLOWER ASSEMBLY AND STEM

1. Attach one end of the #20 stem wire to the toothpick in the mushroom cap with floral tape. Continue taping to the end of the stem. Cut off tape.
2. Using the small artist's paintbrush, paint the inside of the mushroom cap black, leaving the cut-off stem or "flower center" unpainted. Set aside to dry.

THE CREATIVE TOUCH

Combine several mushroom flowers with the Seashell Flowers in this chapter for an unforgettable centerpiece for a traditional home.

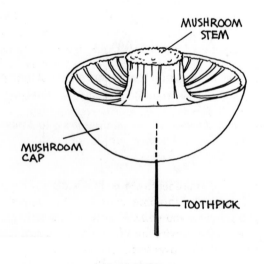

MUSHROOM STEM

MUSHROOM CAP

TOOTHPICK

DIAGRAM A

Pine-Cone Flower

Very conservative or bright and whimsical—the colors for this pine-cone flower are up to you. The bottom half of a pine cone forms the flower petals; the inner row of petals are "feathered" with a knife, then both petal rows painted in contrasting colors. A tiny cotton ball covered with fabric is your flower center. The flower is attached to a stem wire, finished with floral tape.

MATERIALS FOR 1 FLOWER

PETAL UNIT

pine cone with stem
acrylic paint in desired color
acrylic paint in contrasting color to above

FLOWER CENTER

absorbent cotton cosmetics ball
2-inch-square piece silk lining in desired color
#28 spool wire

FLOWER ASSEMBLY AND STEM

#28 spool wire
8-inch piece #18 stem wire
green floral tape
tacky glue

Also: small handsaw; X-acto knife; scissors; wire cutters; small artist's paintbrush

PETAL UNIT

1. Using a small handsaw, cut off the bottom end of the pine cone, as indicated by the dotted line in Diagram A. Discard the top.
2. Feather the inner row of pine-cone petals by making tiny slashes with the X-acto knife, as shown in Diagram B.

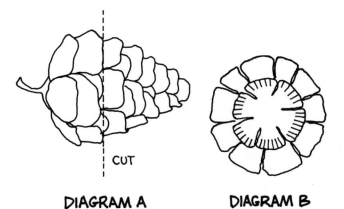

CUT

DIAGRAM A   DIAGRAM B

3. With the small artist's paintbrush, paint the outer row of pine-cone petals inside and out with acrylic paint in desired color. Let dry.
4. Paint the inner row of petals inside and out in the contrasting color. Let dry.

FLOWER CENTER

Divide the absorbent cotton ball into 2 small balls. Cover 1 ball smoothly with the piece of silk lining, drawing the fabric together underneath (Diagram C). Secure it around tightly with a bit of #28 spool wire, but do not cut the wire off the spool. Trim off excess fabric, leaving ¼ inch below wire. (Save the other cotton ball for another flower.)

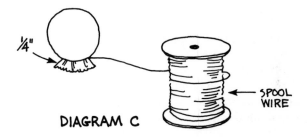

¼"

SPOOL WIRE

DIAGRAM C

FLOWER ASSEMBLY AND STEM

1. Wind the #28 spool wire hanging from the flower center through and around the rows of pine-cone petals, eventually bringing the wire out on the underside of the pine cone, around its stem. Then twist the spool wire to attach the pine cone to one end of the #18 stem wire. Cut the wire from the spool.
2. With the floral tape, cover the spool wire at the base of the pine cone. Continue taping down the length of the stem wire to the end. Cut off tape.
3. Glue the flower center to the exact inside center of the pine cone.

VARIATION

You may omit the flower center and simply paint over the center of the pine cone with the contrasting color. However, you will still need to attach the pine cone to the stem wire by first winding some spool wire through the rows of pine-cone petals.

THE CREATIVE TOUCH

Combine several pine-cone flowers with colorful autumn leaves dried with glycerin and some pampas grass and arrange in a wicker or pine-cone basket. Or paint the flowers red and arrange with holly and other greens for a Christmas decoration.

Tea Rose

This flower is almost indistinguishable from the real thing, a lovely, velvety rose—of wood fiber! Three single and 3 double petal units are folded around and hooked to a long stem wire. A craft calyx is added and the stem finished by taping, adding 2 craft leaves.

The pre-cut, wood-fiber petal units are available in crafts stores.

MATERIALS FOR 1 FLOWER AND 2 LEAVES

PETAL UNITS

9 wood-fiber rose petal units in desired color
white resin glue

FLOWER ASSEMBLY AND STEM

15-inch piece #18 stem wire
#28 covered wire
white resin glue
craft calyx (rose type)
green floral tape
2 craft leaves (rose type)

Also: scissors; toothpicks, wax paper or aluminum foil (for gluing)

PETAL UNITS

1. Glue together 2 petal units; repeat twice to make 3 double petal units.
2. With scissors, slit the double petal units and the 3 remaining single petal units, as indicated by the dotted lines in Diagram A.

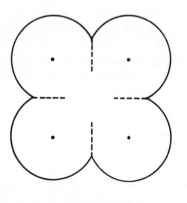

DIAGRAM A

FLOWER ASSEMBLY AND STEM

1. Fold 1 of the single petal units in half, then roll the petal unit toward you in the direction indicated by the arrows in Diagram B. Attach it to one end of the #18 stem wire with the #28 covered wire by wrapping the wire around the base of the petal unit. Cut the wire off very close.

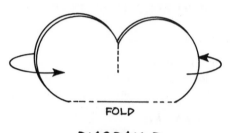

FOLD

DIAGRAM B

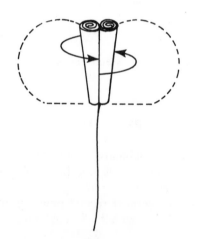

DIAGRAM C

2. Fold a second single petal unit in half and, with the rolled-up petal unit in the center, as shown in Diagram C, roll the second petal unit around the first, as in Step 1. Secure it at the base to the stem wire with the #28 coverd wire. Cut off wire.
3. Wrap the third single petal unit around the first 2 petal units and attach to the stem wire, as in Step 2.
4. With the tip of your scissors, make a tiny hole in

the exact center of each double petal unit. Put a drop of glue on each center hole and push the petal units, one at a time, up the stem wire until they are right under the single petal units. Make sure petal tips are nicely staggered. Put drops of glue on each double petal unit (as indicated by dots in Diagram A), and glue each row of petals to the row above.

5. Push the calyx up the stem wire until it is right under the petal units. Attach to the stem with floral tape. Continue taping down the stem for 4 inches with the floral tape.

6. Attach the first craft leaf to the stem wire with tape. Continue taping another 3 inches down the stem.

7. Attach the second leaf to the stem opposite the first leaf. Continue taping down to the bottom of the stem. Cut off tape.

8. If necessary, reshape the petals by curling.

THE CREATIVE TOUCH

A big bouquet of these handsome, realistic-looking roses is a delightful addition to any home. On occasion we have even dabbed a bit of rose perfume on our arrangement. If you make a large quantity of these flowers, consider varying the sizes by adding or subtracting petal units.

Pompon

A very easy, very informal flower, this pompon is made of fluffy feathers attached to a stem wire. The stem is finished by taping with floral tape, adding 2 green feather leaves.

The feathers are available in a wide variety of colors and lengths in crafts stores.

FLOWER ASSEMBLY AND STEM

1. Make a tiny hook at one end of the #20 stem wire. With the fluffy feathers curving outward, attach them around the hook with the #28 covered wire. Cut the wire off very close.

2. Tape over the covered wire with floral tape, then tape down the stem wire 4 inches.

3. Attach the first green feather to the stem wire with the floral tape. Continue taping another 2 inches down the stem.

4. Attach the second feather-leaf to the stem opposite the first. Continue taping down to the bottom of the stem. Cut off tape.

THE CREATIVE TOUCH

Make several of these pompons for a "campy" container found in a thrift shop or at a flea market. Tuck in tendrils of young ivy to complete the arrangement.

MATERIALS FOR 1 FLOWER AND 2 LEAVES

10-inch piece #20 stem wire
twenty 3-inch fluffy feathers in desired color
#28 covered wire
green floral tape
two 5-inch green feathers (for leaves)

Also: wire cutters; scissors

Miniature Rosebud

This delicate pink rosebud is made of wood-fiber petals. Five petal units cut from a pattern are each folded around a short length of covered wire, then rolled one inside the other to form the bud. The rolled petals are then wired to a stem wire, and a small craft calyx is added. To finish, the stem is covered with floral tape.

MATERIALS FOR 1 FLOWER

PETAL UNITS

sheet of wood fiber in pink
#28 white-covered wire

FLOWER ASSEMBLY AND STEM

green floral tape
6-inch piece #20 stem wire
small craft calyx (rose type)

Also: pencil, tissue paper, scissors; wire cutters

PETAL UNITS

1. Make your tissue paper pattern for the petal unit, tracing from book Pattern 1. Cut 5 petal units out of wood fiber, following Pattern 1.
2. Cut five 6-inch pieces of the #28 covered wire. Bend each one to form a right angle of 4 inches on the horizontal and 2 inches on the vertical.

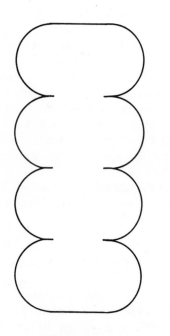

PATTERN 1

3. Fold 1 of the petal units in half, as shown in Diagram A, then fold in half again in the opposite direction around 1 of the bent wires, as shown in Diagram B. Do not gather the petal unit or pull it tight; make sure it is flush against the right angle in the

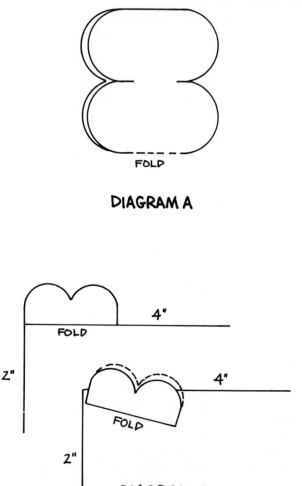

wire. Roll up the petal unit and the covered wire tightly, as indicated by the direction of the arrow in Diagram C, rolling to the end of the wire. Do not cut off the wire "tail" or stem.
4. Repeat Step 3 with a second petal unit and piece of covered wire, except this time roll the petal unit around the first petal unit, gathering the petals slightly and staggering their placement.
5. Repeat Steps 3 and 4 with the remaining petal units and pieces of covered wire.

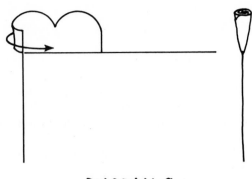

DIAGRAM C

FLOWER ASSEMBLY AND STEM

1. Tape together the dangling "tails" of covered wire, then twist this around one end of the #20 stem wire.

2. Push the calyx up the stem wire until it is right under the petal units; attach to the stem with floral tape. Continue taping down the stem to the end. Cut off tape.

3. Shape the petals by curling.

VARIATION

The same flower can be made with silk lining fabric in the color of your choice, but be sure to apply sizing to the fabric after cutting out the petal units. You may also attach craft leaves (rose type) to the stem wire.

THE CREATIVE TOUCH

Welcome home a new baby with a tiny bassinet filled with miniature rosebuds, fresh baby's breath and maidenhair fern inserted in Oasis. You can buy the bassinet from a florist or make your own out of a plastic container trimmed with lace and pink or blue velvet ribbon.

Seashell Flowers

Two pretty shell flowers—both made by gluing rows of shell "petals" around a button center attached to a stem wire. For the first flower, a craft daisy center is glued to the very center of the button; for the second flower, 3 pearl stamens are used. To finish both, you add a craft calyx, then tape the stem.

MATERIALS FOR FLOWER #1

SHELLS (FLOWER PETALS)

3 large cup-shaped shells
3 small cup-shaped shells
household bleach
glycerin

FLOWER ASSEMBLY AND STEM

15-inch piece #18 stem wire
¾-inch-diameter clear plastic button with 2 holes
Bond's 527 glue
craft flower center (daisy type)
craft calyx (daisy type)
green floral tape

Also: paper towels (for drying shells); sponge or piece of cheesecloth (for polishing shells); tweezers, wax paper or aluminum foil (for gluing); scissors

SHELLS (FLOWER PETALS)

1. Soak shells in bleach, then rinse and dry.
2. With a sponge or piece of cheesecloth, polish the shells on both sides with glycerin.

FLOWER ASSEMBLY AND STEM

1. Hook the #18 stem wire through the holes of the button until about a 2-inch piece appears on the underside of the second hole (Diagram A). Twist the wires together to secure.

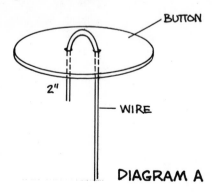

DIAGRAM A

2. Glue the daisy center to the exact center of the button.
3. Apply glue heavily to the button around the daisy center. Using tweezers, glue the smaller shells to the button in an almost upright position, as shown in Diagram B, with the pointed ends of the shells on the button, and overlapping them slightly. Let dry completely.

DIAGRAM B

4. Apply glue heavily to the edge of the button, and glue the larger shells around the first row of shells. Glue in the same almost upright position, overlapping them slightly and staggering their placement around the inner row.
5. Push the calyx up the stem wire until it is right under the button; secure with a drop of glue.
6. With floral tape, start taping near the bottom of the calyx. Continue taping to the end of the stem wire. Cut off tape.

MATERIALS FOR FLOWER #2

SHELLS (FLOWER PETALS)

6 large cup-shaped shells
4 medium-size cup-shaped shells
5 tiny cup-shaped shells
household bleach
glycerin

FLOWER ASSEMBLY AND STEM

10-inch piece #18 stem wire
1-inch-diameter clear plastic button
Bond's 527 glue
3 single pearl craft stamens
craft calyx
green floral tape

Follow all steps as for Flower #1, except substitute the 3 pearl stamens for the craft flower center, and, instead of gluing the shells perpendicular to the button, glue them flat on the button with the concave side up and the curved or rounded ends of the shells on the button. Glue 3 rows of shells, beginning with the tiny shells in the center and working out to the large shells, as shown in Diagram C.

DIAGRAM C

The shells can be tinted by immersing them in a commercial liquid dye (mixed according to package directions) until the desired color is obtained.

THE CREATIVE TOUCH

When we arranged these seashell flowers and the mushroom flowers in this chapter with coral, pampas grass, artificial greenery and wooden cherubs, the combination immediately became a hit in both our homes. The arrangement also works extremely well in a reception room or office, because it goes with any period of interior design.

Miniature Seashell Bouquet

A delicate and lovely mini-bouquet made of shell flowers, snail-shell buds and fish-scale leaves—all attached to stem-wire branches covered with floss. The individual units are assembled with wire and green floss, then combined and arranged in a shell container filled with plaster of Paris.

All of the shells used in the bouquet are available in shell shops, though occasionally certain shells are sold in crafts stores. It is also possible to buy shells with holes already cut in them, in which case you can omit some of the beginning steps given below.

MATERIALS FOR 1 BOUQUET
(30 BUDS, 3 FLOWERS, 10 LEAVES)

BUDS

thirty ¼-inch-wide snail shells
30 pieces #28 spool wire, each 1½ inches long
green cotton floss or silk floss
Bond's 527 glue

PETALS

24 #1 cup-shaped shells
24 pieces #28 spool wire, each 3 inches long

FLOWER ASSEMBLY

6 single craft stamens in desired color
green cotton floss or silk floss
3 pieces #20 stem wire, each 2 inches long
#32 lacing wire
Bond's 527 glue

LEAVES

15 small garfish scales
15 pieces #32 lacing wire, each 2 inches long
green cotton floss or silk floss
Bond's 527 glue

BOUQUET ASSEMBLY

3 pieces #20 stem wire, each 5 inches long
green cotton floss or silk floss
Bond's 527 glue
1-inch-diameter flat shell or piece of beach glass (for container base)
1 medium-size cup-shaped shell (for container)
plaster of Paris

Also: awl, ice pick or pin vise; wire cutters; scissors

BUDS

1. Using an awl, pierce a hole in each of the 30 snail shells (indicated by the dot in Diagram A). Turn the awl slowly and carefully to avoid breaking the shell.

DIAGRAM A

2. Loop a 1½-inch piece of the #28 spool wire through the hole in a snail shell; twist the ends of the wire together to secure. Beginning at the base of the shell, tape down the twisted wire with floss. Secure at the end with a drop of glue. Repeat for the remaining 29 snail shells.

PETALS

1. Using an awl, pierce 2 holes in each #1 cup-shaped shell (indicated by the dots in Diagram B). Again, turn the awl slowly and carefully to avoid breaking the shell. The holes should be ¼ inch apart.

DIAGRAM B

2. Loop a 3-inch piece of #28 spool wire through the 2 holes in a shell. Twist the ends of the wire together to secure. Repeat for the remaining 23 cup-shaped shells.

FLOWER ASSEMBLY

1. With the green cotton floss, tape 2 craft stamens to one end of a 2-inch piece of #20 stem wire. Repeat for the remaining stamens and 2-inch pieces of stem wire.

2. Using the #32 lacing wire, attach 3 cup-shaped shells, concave side up, to one 2-inch piece of stem wire, so that the top of the shell is about ¼ inch below the stamen tips.

3. Right underneath the first row of shells, attach a second row of 5 cup-shaped shells, staggering the placement of the shells. Cut off the lacing wire very close.

4. Beginning just under the shells, tape down the stem wire to the end with floss. Cut off floss and secure at the end with a drop of glue.

5. Repeat Steps 2, 3 and 4 with the remaining cup-shaped shells for 2 more flowers.

LEAVES

1. Using an awl, pierce a hole in each garfish scale (indicated by the dot in Diagram C). Turn the awl slowly and carefully to avoid breaking the scale.

DIAGRAM C

2. Loop a 2-inch piece of #32 lacing wire through the hole in one of the garfish scales. Twist the ends of the wire together to secure. Tape down the lacing wire with floss. Cut off floss at end and secure with a drop of glue.

3. Repeat Step 2 with the remaining 14 garfish scales and 2-inch pieces of lacing wire.

BOUQUET ASSEMBLY

1. Using floss, attach the snail shells (buds) to the three 5-inch pieces of #20 stem wire, distributing the shells among the 3 stems as desired (Diagram D). Cut off floss and secure with glue.

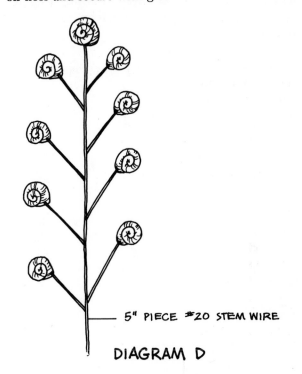

5" PIECE #20 STEM WIRE

DIAGRAM D

2. Using floss, attach the garfish scales (leaves) to the 6 pieces of #20 stem wire (the 3 branches of snail-shell buds and the 3 flower stems).

3. For the container, glue the small flat shell to the underside of the medium-size cup-shaped shell.

4. Mix the plaster of Paris according to the directions on the package, then pour into the shell container. While the mixture is still wet, insert the 3 stems with the buds, flowers and leaves in a suitable arrangement.

THE CREATIVE TOUCH

For a fanciful vanity accent piece, paint the shell container with pearlized nail polish in the color of your choice. This is the perfect hostess gift for someone who loves shells.

Seashell Wreath

This exquisite natural wreath is composed of things from the sea and shore—shells, bits of coral, sand dollars and other materials—along with different dried flowers. The Seashell Flowers from this chapter are also included. A styrofoam ring wound with brown satin ribbon forms the base.

MATERIALS FOR 1 WREATH

WREATH BASE

10-inch-diameter rounded styrofoam ring
2½ yards 2-inch-wide brown satin ribbon
white resin glue
24-inch piece of picture wire

DECORATIVE MATERIALS

assortment of shells and other ocean articles, such as sand dollars, sea horses, starfish, bits of coral
6 to 10 Seashell Flowers (page 106)
about 100 2½-inch wired floral picks
50 to 75 small sprigs dried statice
few sprigs other dried flowers, such as skyrocket, wheat or yarrow

Also: scissors; wire cutters; ice pick

WREATH BASE

1. Wind the styrofoam ring with the satin ribbon, securing at both ends with glue.
2. Attach the picture wire to the wreath by wrapping it around as shown in Diagram A, twisting to secure. Cut away excess wire.

DECORATIVE MATERIALS

1. With an ice pick, pierce holes in all the individual shells, as indicated in Diagram B. Loop a wire at the end of a floral pick to secure, as shown in Diagram C. Repeat for all individual shells, ocean articles, and all shell flowers.
2. Attach the small sprigs of statice to wired floral picks.
3. Attach the few sprigs of other dried flowers to wired floral picks.

WREATH ASSEMBLY

1. Attach the statice sprigs to the wreath by pushing the floral picks into the styrofoam.
2. After the wreath is completely covered with statice, attach the individual shells, ocean articles, and the shell flowers wherever desired.
3. Attach the remaining dried flowers to the wreath.

THE CREATIVE TOUCH

When designing this beautiful wreath (it could sell for more than two hundred dollars in a boutique!), be sure to coordinate the colors of shells and dried plant material; also, we suggest you use fairly subtle colors. We believe this is one project that is destined to become a treasured family heirloom. Simply refurbish the wreath every few years with new dried plant material and add special seashells as you acquire them.

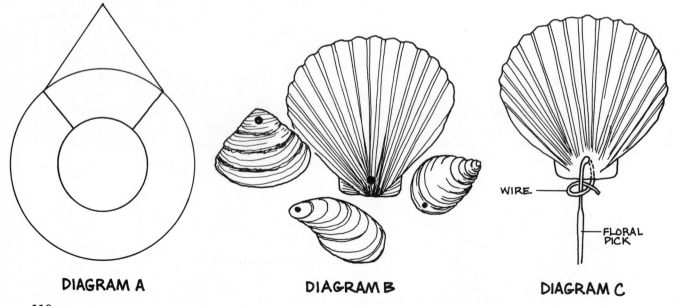

DIAGRAM A   DIAGRAM B   DIAGRAM C

SEVEN

Flowers from Throwaways

This is our not-quite-so-serious chapter in which we give in to the little bit of squirrel in us by turning throwaway items we can't bear to part with into perfectly marvelous flowers. From the humble origins of egg carton, aluminum soft-drink can and old glove emerge such beauties as forget-me-nots, poppies and cattails.

Scatter these novelty flowers throughout the house wherever you would like a surefire conversation piece. Your ecology-conscious friends will applaud you for not littering the landscape, and the rest of your friends and family will admire your cleverness.

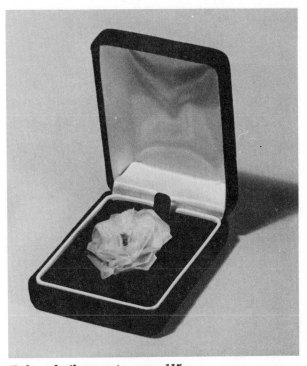

Fish-scale flower pin, page 115

Cornhusk flower, page 114

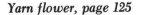

Oriental poppy, page 122

Yarn flower, page 125

Above, two plastic flowers, page 121

Egg carton rose, page 124

Forget-me-nots, page 116

Cattail, page 113

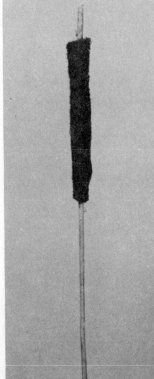

Pansy pin, page 119

Cattail

Transform a lonely old glove into a brand-new flower—cut an oval out of a brown leather glove or patch of suede, following our simple pattern. Apply some glue to the wrong side of your cutout piece, then roll it tightly around one end of a long stem wire taped with floral tape.

MATERIALS FOR 1 CATTAIL

old brown leather glove or suede patch
12-inch piece #18 stem wire
green floral tape
tacky glue

Also: pencil, tissue paper, scissors

CATTAIL ASSEMBLY AND STEM

1. Make a tissue paper pattern, tracing from book Pattern 1. Cut a piece out of the glove, following Pattern 1.

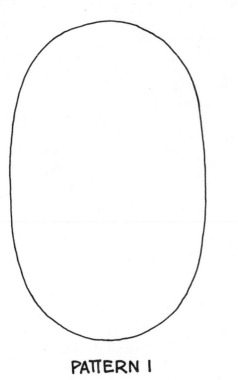

PATTERN 1

2. Tape down the entire length of the #18 stem wire with floral tape. Cut off tape.

3. Apply glue to the wrong side of the cutout leather piece. Roll the piece tightly around one end of the stem wire, as indicated by the arrows in Diagram A, leaving a ½-inch piece of stem wire exposed at the tip.

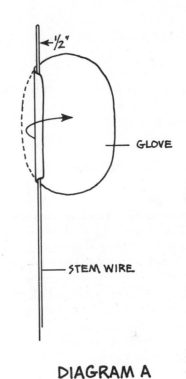

DIAGRAM A

THE CREATIVE TOUCH

These cattails combine very well with the Feathery Flowers in Chapter Six and some dried weeds. For the container, consider a duck decoy, and give the whole ensemble to your favorite man for his office or study.

Cornhusk Flower

Give the summertime task of husking corn a dual purpose—long after the barbecue or picnic, the saved cornhusk leaves can be used to make delightful flowers for your home. Flower petals are cut from a pattern out of the cornhusk leaves, then glued in staggered rows around a rust-painted seedpod center attached to a stem wire. The edges and inner sides of the petals are painted a coordinating color.

MATERIALS FOR 1 FLOWER

PETALS

3 to 4 dried cornhusk leaves or craft cornhusk leaves
½ cup household bleach
2 tablespoons glycerin

PETALS

1. Fill a 3-quart kettle with lukewarm water and ½ cup household bleach and immerse the cornhusk leaves for 2 to 3 hours. Remove husks and spread out on newspaper to dry in the sun.
2. Fill a bowl with water and 2 tablespoons glycerin and immerse the husks in the solution for 1 hour.
3. While the husks are soaking, make a cardboard pattern for a petal from book Pattern 1. Remove husks from the glycerin and water solution and, laying the cardboard pattern on the wet husks, cut out 18 petals. Set petals aside.

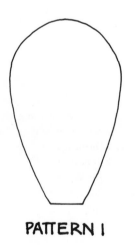

PATTERN 1

FLOWER CENTER

For the flower center, spray the seedpod with rust or reddish brown acrylic paint.

FLOWER CENTER

seedpod from sweet gum tree (or ball fringe, dried cloverhead or small thistlehead)
acrylic spray paint in rust or reddish brown

FLOWER ASSEMBLY AND STEM

10-inch piece #16 stem wire
green floral tape
clear craft cement
acrylic or watercolor paint in desired color
2-inch-diameter paper cup

Also: 3-quart kettle, newspaper, bowl; pencil, tissue paper, cardboard, scissors; small artist's paintbrush

FLOWER ASSEMBLY AND STEM

1. Attach the flower center to one end of the #16 stem wire with floral tape. Continue taping to the end of the stem wire. Cut off tape.
2. Dip the narrow end of a damp petal into clear craft cement and attach it to the flower center slightly above the halfway point, as shown in Diagram A. Repeat with 6 more petals to complete a row of evenly spaced petals.
3. Immediately below the first row, attach the remaining 11 petals to form a second row, making sure to stagger the placement of the petals.
4. While still wet, shape the flower by inserting it upside down in a paper cup until dry.

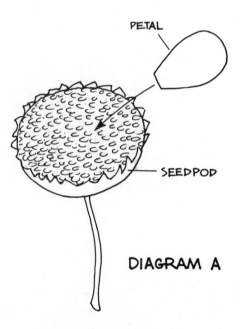

PETAL

SEEDPOD

DIAGRAM A

5. When completely dry, paint the edges and the inner sides of the petals near the flower center, using a small artist's paintbrush and acrylic or watercolor paint.

THE CREATIVE TOUCH

For a fabulous centerpiece for the dining table, one that is also edible, arrange cornhusk flowers in a wicker basket with small loaves of French or Italian bread, rolls and bagels. For foliage, shred wet cornhusks with a pin and attach to floral picks, then insert in the centerpiece. We painted our flowers pumpkin orange and tied matching velvet bows to the basket handle.

To make the centerpiece more permanent, bake the breads in a 225° oven for 8 hours. When cool, spray the breads with a clear gloss varnish.

Fish-Scale Flower Pin

This unusual "seaflower" pin is made of different-sized ocean fish scales glued in petal rows on a small plastic circular base. A skyrocket or other tiny dried natural flower is glued to the very center. Finish by attaching a bar-pin back to the underside of the pin.

MATERIALS FOR 1 FLOWER PIN

FISH SCALES (FLOWER PETALS)

25 to 35 ocean fish scales in 2 sizes (about 1/3 of the scales should be the size of your smallest fingernail; the rest of the scales should be the size of the nail on your ring finger)

FLOWER PIN ASSEMBLY

Bond's 527 glue
¾-inch-diameter plastic circle or clear plastic button
tiny dried flower, such as a skyrocket
½-inch to ¾-inch bar-pin back

Also: knife, 1-quart pot or pan, aluminum foil; tweezers

FISH SCALES (FLOWER PETALS)

After scaling the fish with a knife, prepare the fish scales: Stir 1 tablespoon of salt into 1 quart of water and soak the fish scales in the solution for 1 hour. Spread the fish scales on a piece of aluminum foil to dry.

FLOWER PIN ASSEMBLY

1. Using tweezers to pick up the fish scales, dip the narrower end of the smaller scales into glue and attach these around the center of the plastic circle in a single row. The scales should be nearly upright, as shown in Diagram A.

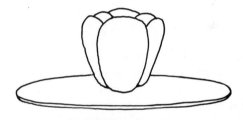

DIAGRAM A

2. Repeat Step 1 for the larger fish scales, making as many rows as necessary to cover the plastic circle, staggering the placement of the scales from one row to the next.

3. Glue the dried flower to the exact center of the pin.

4. Glue the bar-pin back to the underside of the pin.

VARIATIONS

Glue the fish scales flat onto the plastic circle instead of standing them upright, and work from the circumference to the center.

If you want the pin to have a color other than the natural off-white color of the fish scales, add a small amount of glass stain in the desired color to the solution of salt and water.

THE CREATIVE TOUCH

Save a jewelry box lined with velveteen or satin for this lovely pin so you can bestow it on a favorite person with style.

115

Forget-Me-Nots

As if by magic, a couple of empty egg cartons can become a charming bouquet of spring flowers . . . petal units are cut from a pattern out of the flat part of one carton; tiny circles are cut out of a contrasting-color carton for the flower centers. A piece of stem wire is looped through 2 holes punched in each petal unit, the stem then finished by twisting the wire ends together and covering with floral tape. Flower centers are simply glued in place.

Natural forget-me-nots come in pale pink, light blue or white—we have used light blue for ours.

PATTERN I

MATERIALS FOR 12 FLOWERS

PETAL UNITS

plastic egg carton in light blue

FLOWER CENTERS

plastic egg carton in contrasting color to above

FLOWER ASSEMBLY AND STEM

12 pieces #20 stem wire, each 6 inches long
white resin glue
green floral tape

Also: pencil, tissue paper, scissors; ice pick or awl; ruler, compass

PETAL UNITS

Make your tissue paper pattern, tracing from book Pattern 1. Cut 12 petal units out of the flat part of the blue egg carton, following Pattern 1.

FLOWER CENTERS

1. With a ruler and compass, mark off a ⅜-inch-diameter circle on tissue paper and cut out. This will be your pattern for the flower center.
2. Using your pattern, cut 12 flower centers out of the contrasting-color carton.

FLOWER ASSEMBLY AND STEM

1. With the ice pick, make 2 tiny holes ¼ inch apart in the center of each petal unit.
2. Loop a piece of the #20 stem wire through the holes in a petal unit. Twist the ends of the wire together underneath to secure. Repeat with the remaining petal units and pieces of #20 stem wire.
3. Glue a flower center to the top center of each petal unit.
4. Beginning just underneath each flower, tape down the length of the stem wires with floral tape. Cut off tape.

THE CREATIVE TOUCH

For a novel centerpiece at Easter time, arrange several forget-me-nots with plastic eggs and artificial parsley in an attractive casserole dish. Or for individual place settings, place the flowers and a little greenery in your prettiest egg cups.

Jewelry Flowers

Here is an excellent technique for refurbishing old or broken jewelry. To make a decorative miniature bouquet of flowers: with wire cutters, separate the flowers from the main jewelry pieces; paint the flowers with acrylic paints, if needed. For stems and foliage, use pieces of #32 gold lacing wire and form into loops and twists. Join the flower and foliage pieces with liquid solder and assemble in a tiny flowerpot or vase. Use another throwaway item, such as a toothpaste cap, for the vase, and fill it with floral clay. For a variation, paint the finished arrangement all over with gold paint to achieve the effect of vermeil.

MATERIALS FOR 1 MINIATURE FLORAL ARRANGEMENT

FIRST STEPS

old or broken flower jewelry (the pin we used had
⅜-inch-diameter flowers)
#26 spool wire
3 to 5 pieces #32 gold lacing wire, each 4 inches long

ASSEMBLY

liquid solder
miniature vase (the one we used was approximately
¾ inch tall)

Also: wire cutters

FIRST STEPS

1. Separate the flowers from the rest of the jewelry with wire cutters (Diagram A).

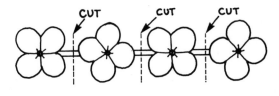

DIAGRAM A

2. For flower stems, cut as many pieces of the #26 spool wire as you have flowers. These should measure about 1 inch, with the lengths varying slightly.

3. For foliage, fold in half the pieces of #32 gold lacing wire. Make a tiny loop at the folded end of one

of the wire pieces, then proceed to twist the wires together and make 4 to 5 additional loops as you go (Diagram B). Repeat the step with the remaining pieces of gold lacing wire, making sure to vary the placement of the loops on each one.

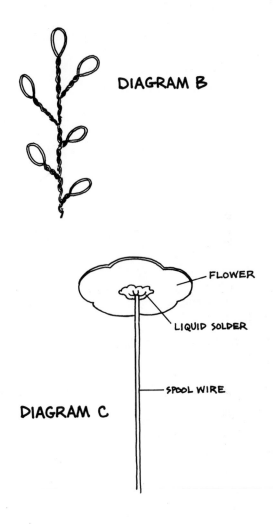

ASSEMBLY

1. Attach each flower to a short piece of spool wire by dabbing liquid solder on the back of the flower and pushing the wire into it (Diagram C). Let the solder dry with the flowers upside down.
2. Arrange the flowers and the foliage in the vase.

THE CREATIVE TOUCH

These miniature, Fabergé-like arrangements add an elegant note to both dollhouse and real house. We like to display these on small occasional tables or on a vanity.

May Blossoms

Another easy trick—a dozen pretty blossoms are formed by cutting out and shaping the cups from a plastic egg carton! Three craft stamens taped to a piece of stem wire are inserted through the center of each petal unit, the stem finished with tape.

MATERIALS FOR 12 FLOWERS

PETAL UNITS

plastic egg carton in desired color

FLOWER ASSEMBLY AND STEM

36 single craft stamens in desired color
12 pieces #20 stem wire, each 4 inches long
green floral tape

Also: scissors

PETAL UNITS

1. Cut the egg cups out of the carton.
2. Cut each cup to form 4 petals, as shown in Diagram A, rounding off the tips of the petals as indicated by the dotted lines.

FLOWER ASSEMBLY AND STEM

1. Using floral tape, take 3 stamens and attach them to one end of a piece of #20 stem wire.
2. With the tip of your scissors, make a tiny hole in the exact center of a petal unit. Put the bottom end of the #20 stem wire down through the hole and push the petal unit up the stem until it is right under the stamens.
3. Beginning just beneath the flower, tape down the length of stem wire with floral tape. Cut off tape.
4. Repeat Steps 1 to 3 with the remaining stamens, stem wires and petal units to make a dozen flowers.

THE CREATIVE TOUCH

Add a bit of spring to a guest bedroom or powder room by arranging a bouquet of these flowers in different pastel colors in a white procelain container. Combine with sprigs of baby's breath and some greenery.

DIAGRAM A

Pansy Pin

Make a pretty pansy pin from a piece of old leather! Five flower petals and a leaf unit are cut out of leather, following simple patterns. Petals are soaked in water and shaped while wet and pliable, then pinned into shape to dry. To assemble, the leather cutouts are glued together, then painted in bright colors of acrylic paint. Glue a bar-pin back to the underside, and spray with acrylic sealer to finish.

MATERIALS FOR 1 PIN (1 FLOWER AND 2 LEAVES)

FLOWER PETALS AND LEAF UNIT

5 × 6-inch piece of old, soft leather
styrofoam block or cork disk

PIN ASSEMBLY

clear craft cement
½-inch to ¾-inch bar-pin back
acrylic paints in a light and a dark shade of purple, and yellow, white and green
spray acrylic sealer in gloss finish

Also: pencil, tissue paper, scissors; straight pins; small artist's paintbrush

FLOWER PETALS AND LEAF UNIT

1. Make your tissue paper pattern for a petal, tracing from book Pattern 1. Cut 5 petals out of the leather, following Pattern 1.
2. Make your tissue paper pattern for the leaf unit, tracing from book Pattern 2. Cut a leaf unit out of the leather, following Pattern 2. Set aside.
3. Soak the 5 leather petals in a cup of warm water for ½ hour.

4. Remove the petals from the water and, while wet and pliable, pinch and push them to resemble the shape of pansy petals; use a straight pin to help ruffle the petal edges. Pin the petals to a block of styrofoam, propping them with pins where necessary to hold their shape (Diagram A). Let the petals dry completely before removing the pins.

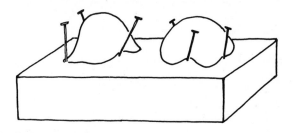

DIAGRAM A

PIN ASSEMBLY

1. Put a drop of clear craft cement on the underside of the narrow ends of the petals and glue them to the center of the leaf unit, overlapping them slightly.
2. Glue the bar-pin back to the underside of the leaf unit.
3. Using a small artist's paintbrush, paint the flower petals a light shade of purple. When completely dry, highlight the flower with yellow, white and deep purple.
4. Paint the leaf unit green.
5. Spray the entire pin with acrylic sealer.

THE CREATIVE TOUCH

Reduce the size of the patterns and make a pair of matching earrings. We can't think of a nicer Mother's Day present!

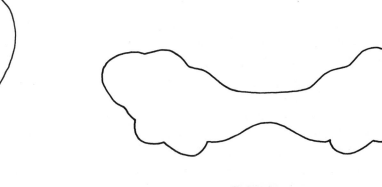

PATTERN 1

PATTERN 2

Party Favor Flower

Remodel that worn, neglected flower pin that is taking up space in your jewelry box into a lovely miniature flower in a lace-trimmed pot. Remove the pin backing; paint the flower and front of pin in bright colors. Cover the stem with satin tubing and insert into a styrofoam-filled flowerpot (we used a painted cosmetic bottle cap for our container). Trim the pot with a bit of lace and add a tiny satin bow.

MATERIALS FOR 1 MINIATURE FLOWER AND FLOWERPOT

FIRST STEPS

costume jewelry pin of flower with stem
acrylic paint in desired color
acrylic paint in contrasting color
cosmetic bottle cap (we used a 1-inch-diameter cap, 1¼ inches tall)

FLOWER AND FLOWERPOT ASSEMBLY

satin tubing in desired color (available at fabric stores; we used a 7-inch piece of tubing, ¼ inch in diameter)
small piece styrofoam
dried sheet moss
white resin glue
2-inch piece #20 stem wire
3-inch piece lace in desired color
#28 covered wire in desired color

Also: wire cutters; small artist's paintbrushes; toothpicks (for gluing)

FIRST STEPS

1. With wire cutters, remove the bar-pin back from the pin.
2. Paint the petals of the pin in the desired color; paint the edges and center of the pin in the contrasting color. Set aside to dry.
3. Paint the cosmetic bottle cap in the contrasting color. Set aside to dry.

FLOWER AND FLOWERPOT ASSEMBLY

1. Cut a 1-inch piece out of the satin tubing. Set aside.
2. Fill the bottle cap with styrofoam and cover the styrofoam with dried moss.
3. Put glue on the stem of the pin and on 1 inch of the #20 stem wire and insert both in the 1-inch piece of tubing; the unglued portion of stem wire should be protruding from the tubing at the other end, opposite the flower. Let dry completely.
4. Push the end of the stem wire not covered by satin tubing into the styrofoam; see Diagram A, in which the dotted line represents the stem wire.
5. Cut the lace in half lengthwise and glue 1 piece around the top edge of the bottle cap.
6. Tie the remaining piece of satin tubing into a bow with knotted ends and attach just under the flower with #28 covered wire.

THE CREATIVE TOUCH

These miniature potted flowers make perfect party favors for a little girl's birthday.

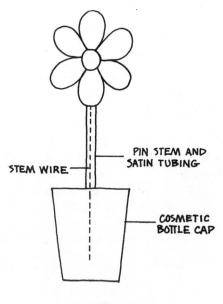

STEM WIRE — PIN STEM AND SATIN TUBING

COSMETIC BOTTLE CAP

DIAGRAM A

Plastic Flowers

Instead of throwing out those tacky plastic posies, try one of the following procedures to turn ordinary plastic flowers into something spectacular. Three simple formulas are given—one to create a lovely, rich bouquet of dark-colored flowers; two different options for all-white arrangements.

FORMULA #1—MATERIALS FOR DARK-COLORED FLOWERS

2 tablespoons varnish
2 tablespoons turpentine
2 tablespoons mahogany stain
⅛ teaspoon burnt umber
⅛ teaspoon black oil paint
bunch of plastic flowers in desired color
styrofoam block

Also: large jar with lid; small artist's paintbrush or sponge, paper towels

1. In a large jar, mix the first 5 ingredients well. The mixture will keep for several months if stored in a cool place.
2. Brush or sponge the mixture onto the plastic flowers and foliage, then wipe off with a paper towel to obtain a textured appearance. Stand the flowers in the styrofoam block and let dry for 24 hours.

FORMULA #2—MATERIALS FOR WHITE FLOWERS

bunch of white plastic flowers
white enamel paint
styrofoam block
spray acrylic sealer in high gloss finish

Also: small artist's paintbrush

1. Separate the flowers from the foliage and paint them with the white enamel paint. Stand the flowers upright in the styrofoam block until completely dry.

2. Stand the leaves or foliage upright in the styrofoam block and spray both flowers and leaves with acrylic sealer; let dry. Repeat for 2 more coats, letting dry between coats.

FORMULA #3—MATERIALS FOR WHITE FLOWERS

bunch of white plastic flowers
1 pint turpentine
1 pint clear varnish in gloss finish
¼ pint white enamel paint
styrofoam block

Also: metal paint bucket or other throwaway container; clothespins, newspaper; small artist's paintbrush

1. Separate the flowers from the foliage.
2. Mix the turpentine and varnish in a paint bucket. Dip the foliage into the mixture and hang upside down on a clothesline to dry; place some newspaper underneath to catch the drip.
3. Add the white enamel paint to the original mixture and paint each flower. Stand flowers upright in the styrofoam block to dry.

THE CREATIVE TOUCH

Recently we spruced up some old blue plastic anemones and arranged them in a white wicker wall basket for a blue, yellow and white kitchen.

We like Formula #2 above for smaller blossoms such as lilies of the valley; it's very easy and gives the flowers the look of enamel. Last summer we applied Formula #3 above to a large bunch of plastic petunias, then arranged them in an old fireplace grate which we had painted white and put the arrangement on our patio.

Oriental Poppy

Save a couple of 12-ounce soft aluminum cans to make a bright red poppy. Petal units, leaves and calyx are cut from patterns out of the aluminum, then painted. The flower center is made of painted aluminum-foil circles. Flower parts are assembled onto a piece of #20 stem wire, the stem strengthened with additional wire and taped with floral tape.

MATERIALS FOR 1 FLOWER AND 2 LEAVES

PETAL UNITS, LEAVES, CALYX

two 12-ounce soft aluminum cans
spray enamel paint in red
acrylic paint in green

FLOWER CENTER

aluminum foil
acrylic paints in black and yellow

FLOWER ASSEMBLY AND STEM

12-inch piece #20 stem wire
floral adhesive
6-inch piece #18 stem wire
green floral tape

Also: pair of old scissors or tin snips; pencil, tissue paper, compass; ice pick or awl; small artist's paintbrush

PETAL UNITS, LEAVES, CALYX

1. Wash the cans thoroughly and dry inside and out. With the tip of your scissors, make a tiny hole in each can, as shown in Diagram A. With a pair of old scissors or, preferably, tin snips, cut the tops off the cans, as indicated by the dotted line in Diagram A. Cut down the sides of the cans along the seam and cut away the bottoms. Trim away any remaining ragged edges until you have 2 neat rectangular pieces.

2. Flatten the rectangular pieces by bending in the opposite direction from the original shape and pressing under a suitable weight.

3. Make separate tissue paper patterns, tracing from book Patterns 1, 2, 3 and 4.

4. Cut 2 petal units out of the aluminum following Pattern 1; cut 1 petal unit following Pattern 2; cut 2 leaves following Pattern 3; cut 1 calyx following Pattern 4.

5. With the ice pick, make 2 tiny holes ¼ inch apart in the center of each petal unit and in the center of the calyx.

6. With a small artist's paintbrush, paint the petal units on both sides with red enamel paint.

7. Paint both sides of the calyx and the leaves green.

FLOWER CENTER

1. With a compass, draw two 1½-inch-diameter circles on aluminum foil and cut out.

2. Fringe the edges of the foil circles by slashing with scissors.

3. With the tip of your scissors, make 2 tiny holes ¼ inch apart in the center of each circle.

4. Paint both sides of the flower center pieces black. When dry, add a dot of yellow paint to the center of 1 circular piece on one side only.

FLOWER ASSEMBLY AND STEM

1. Push the #20 stem wire through one hole in the calyx, the 2 large petal units, the small petal unit, and the 2 flower centers; the flower center with the yellow dot should be last, with the dot facing up. Loop the stem wire back through the second hole in the flower centers, the small petal unit, the large units, and the calyx, bringing the end back down to the bottom of the stem wire.

2. Before taping the stem wire, put a small amount of floral adhesive between the calyx and the bottom petal unit.

3. Pull the ends of the #20 stem wire taut and place alongside them the piece of #18 stem wire; these will be taped together for an extra-strong stem. Start-

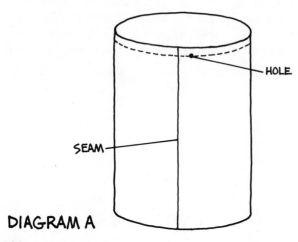

DIAGRAM A

ing right under the calyx, begin taping with floral tape and tape down the stem for 4 inches.

4. Attach the first leaf to the stem with tape. Continue taping down the stem another 2 inches; attach the second leaf to the stem opposite the first leaf.

5. Finish taping to the end of the stem. Cut off tape.

THE CREATIVE TOUCH

Combine a dozen or so poppies with dried eucalyptus and arrange in a black wrought-iron container or an old piece of crockery painted with flat black paint. Another idea is to plant the poppy stems in the soil of some ivy or philodendron.

PATTERN 1

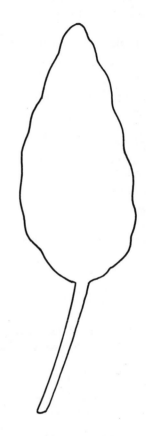

PATTERN 3

PATTERN 2

PATTERN 4

Egg Carton Rose

With a quick touch of your scissors, transform a lowly egg carton into a beautiful rose. Petal units are cutout and shaped egg cups that are drawn up around a cluster of stamens taped to a long stem wire. The stem is covered with green velvet tubing, adding in 5 velvet craft leaves.

MATERIALS FOR 1 FLOWER AND 5 LEAVES

PETAL UNITS

plastic egg carton in desired color
transparent tape

FLOWER ASSEMBLY AND STEM

cluster of single craft stamens in contrasting color
    to above
14-inch piece #20 stem wire
green floral tape
white resin glue
14-inch piece green velvet tubing (available at crafts
    stores)
5 velvet craft leaves

Also: découpage or manicure scissors

DIAGRAM A

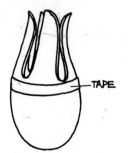

TAPE

DIAGRAM B

PETAL UNITS

1. Cut 4 egg cups out of the carton and cut away each cup to form petals, as shown in Diagram A.
2. Squeeze 1 petal unit gently so petals almost overlap. Wrap around with transparent tape to hold (Diagram B).

FLOWER ASSEMBLY AND STEM

1. Attach the stamen cluster to one end of the #20 stem wire with floral tape.
2. With the tip of your scissors, make a tiny hole in the exact center of each petal unit. Put the stem wire through the holes in each petal unit until the stamens are snug against the last petal unit added, which must be the one that is taped. Be sure to stagger the placement of the petals.
3. Beginning just beneath the flower, build up the stem wire with floral tape for about 1 inch down the stem. Cut off tape.
4. Coat the rest of the stem wire with glue and push the velvet tubing onto the stem wire.
5. With découpage scissors, make 5 holes in the tubing where the craft leaves are desired.
6. Dip the stems of the leaves into glue and then insert the stems in the holes of the tubing, letting no part of the stems show.

THE CREATIVE TOUCH

Place a single rose in a wine bottle or a soft-drink bottle that has been painted or covered with fabric. Craft teachers will love this project, for the rose is so easy and inexpensive to make.

Yarn Flower

This flower provides the perfect way to use left-over yarn. Lengths of coiled wire are bent to form the basic petal shapes or "frames"; colored yarn is then wound around each coil frame for your finished petal. The leaf is made in the same way, winding with green yarn. Assemble the petals around a pompon flower center attached to a long stem wire. Simply tape down the stem to finish, taping in the leaf as you go.

MATERIALS FOR 1 FLOWER AND 1 LEAF

PETALS

5 pieces #28 green-covered wire, each 14 inches long
#2 knitting needle
3 yards mohair yarn in desired color

LEAF

10-inch piece #28 green-covered wire
#2 knitting needle (see above)
18-inch piece mohair yarn in green

FLOWER CENTER

1½ yards mohair yarn in complementary color

FLOWER ASSEMBLY AND STEM

12-inch piece #18 stem wire
#28 green-covered wire
green floral tape

Also: 1-inch-wide ruler, scissors

PETALS

1. Wrap 12 inches of one of the 14-inch pieces of covered wire around the knitting needle, pushing the wire together to form tight coils, and leaving 1 inch hanging on either end (Diagram A).

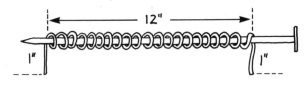

DIAGRAM A

2. Slip the wire off the needle and bring both ends together to form a petal "frame," twisting together the 1-inch ends to secure (Diagram B).

DIAGRAM B

3. Repeat Steps 1 and 2 with the remaining 4 pieces of covered wire to make a total of 5 petal frames.

4. Starting at the base of one of the petal frames, wind back and forth around the wire with the yarn in the desired color, winding the yarn around the inside of the coils as you go (Diagram C). When you reach the top of the petal, wind back down the petal, still winding the yarn around the inside of the coils. Cut off yarn, leaving about 2 inches at the end. Repeat this step for the remaining 4 petals.

DIAGRAM C

LEAF

Repeat Steps 1, 2 and 4 above, as for petals, this time wrapping 8 inches of the 10-inch piece of #28 covered wire around the knitting needle, winding with the green yarn.

FLOWER CENTER

1. For the flower center, wrap yarn in a complementary color around a 1-inch-wide ruler 25 times, or until the desired fullness is reached. Slip the yarn off the ruler and tie together as indicated in Diagram D with a short piece of the same yarn.

2. With scissors, cut across the other end of the yarn, as indicated by the dotted line in Diagram D, and fan into a pompon. Trim to size, if necessary.

FLOWER ASSEMBLY AND STEM

1. Make a small hook in one end of the #18 stem wire and hook around the pompon flower center.

2. With additional #28 covered wire, attach the petals around the flower center to the stem wire.

3. Beginning just beneath the petals, tape over the covered wire with floral tape. Continue taping down the stem wire for 4 inches. Attach the leaf to the stem with tape and finish taping to the end of the stem. Cut off tape.

THE CREATIVE TOUCH

We show our yarn flowers tucked into a live plant in a whimsical ceramic container which resembles a lamb.

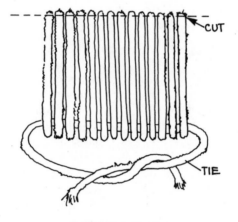

DIAGRAM D

EIGHT:

Flowers from Beads and Other Miscellany

Craft books often end with a chapter of miscellany, and ours is no exception. Except for the flowers made with beads, the projects here defy categorization. But from the Fabergé-like iris to the glistening French dahlia to the mod daisy, the flowers are every bit as impressive as those elsewhere in the book; we wouldn't dream of leaving out a single one!

Several flowers in this chapter require a rudimentary knowledge of the crafts of beading and of needlepoint. We provide you with a quick course in beading in Chapter Two, but if you still run into trouble, you may have to refer to one of several fine books in print on the subject. Likewise with the sole needlepoint project; we have tried to explain it clearly and adequately, but if you have never been exposed to needlepoint, you will probably need a basic instruction book, which you can check out of your library.

Beaded French dahlia, page 132

Needlepoint flower, page 143

Mod daisy, page 134

Cactus

A colorful cactus plant in bloom—all done with beading: 2 large cactus petals made of wound rows of green beads; many, many burrs, each made of 3 short lengths of twisted wire; 4 flowers made of beaded petals laced together, with yellow bead stamens at their center!

MATERIALS FOR 1 PLANT

2 bunches of 11° beads in green
#26 green spool wire
#28 green spool wire
1 bunch 11° beads in desired color
#32 lacing wire in silver or gold

1 strand 11° beads in yellow
4 pieces #16 stem wire, each 6 inches long
green floral tape
cotton batting (or nylon stockings or pantyhose)

Also: small ruler; wire cutters; scissors

CACTUS PETALS

1. For one side of the larger cactus petal, string 5 strands of green beads onto the #26 spool wire. Establish a basic row of 1 inch, and around this wind the beads for a total of 33 rows, rounding the top of the petal and making a point at the bottom. Repeat for the other side of the petal.

2. For one side of the smaller cactus petal, string 4½ strands of green beads onto the #26 spool wire. Establish a basic row of 1 inch, and around this wind the beads for a total of 27 rows, rounding the top of petal and making a point at the bottom. Repeat for the other side of the petal.

BURRS

For each cactus burr, cut three 2½-inch pieces of #28 spool wire. Holding the 3 wires together, push them between 2 rows on the right side of one of the cactus petals wherever desired, then bring the wires back out to the same side after straddling one of the rows, and twist the wires together twice to secure. Cut the wires to a length of ½ inch and fan out. Repeat the entire step for approximately 70 burrs on the larger petal and 50 burrs on the smaller petal, covering the petals with the burrs in an allover random fashion.

FLOWERS

1. For 1 flower petal, string 1 strand of beads in the desired color onto a 5-inch piece of #32 lacing wire. Make a 2-inch loop at one end of the wire and twist to secure, then remove all beads in excess of ⅝ inch, as shown in Diagram A. Repeat the step for 4 more flower petals. Narrow upper petals, then lace together the ⅝-inch portion below each petal to form

a single flower; fan out the petals. Twist together the naked wires below the beads and tape with floral tape to form a single stem.

2. Repeat Step 1 for 3 more flowers, making a total of 4 flowers.

STAMENS

1. For 1 stamen, cut a 4½-inch piece of #32 lacing wire, and push a single yellow bead to the exact center of the wire, then fold the wire in half and twist together to the end (Diagram B). Repeat for 11 more stamens, making a total of 12 stamens.

2. Attach 3 stamens to each flower by pushing the wire ends into the laced-together petal bases.

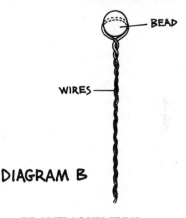

BEAD

WIRES

DIAGRAM B

PLANT ASSEMBLY

1. To provide each cactus petal with support, lay one of the #16 stem wires vertically on the wrong side of the petal so it covers about ¾ of the petal's length; using floral tape, attach the stem wire to the wire at the petal base left over from the beading, but do not tape the end. Repeat for the remaining 3 petals.

2. Fit together the wrong sides of 2 cactus petals that are the same size and stitch the edges together with #32 lacing wire by weaving the wire in and out of the outside 2 rows of beads; leave a 1½-inch opening at the very top and twist the wire to secure. Cut off any excess wire. Repeat for the other 2 petals.

3. Stuff the cotton batting through the openings in the tops of both cactus petals, then stitch the openings together with #32 lacing wire.

4. Attach 2 flowers to the top of the larger cactus petal and 2 flowers to the top of the smaller petal by pushing the flower stems into the petals between stitches.

THE CREATIVE TOUCH

Arrange the plant in a small flowerpot filled with nonhardening floral clay and press into the clay a layer of sand or crushed white stones.

2"

⅝"

DIAGRAM A

Pendo Flower Necklace

This lovely necklace was invented by Patricia Nimocks.

An easy-to-make seashell flower accessory. Flower parts, buds and leaves are shaped out of bright-colored, fast-drying Pendo clay, the clay pieces then assembled and glued between 2 lengths of woven braid. Simply spray your necklace with acrylic sealer to finish, and let dry overnight.

MATERIALS FOR 1 NECKLACE

CLAY FLOWERS, BUDS AND LEAVES

1 package Pendo decorative clay in desired colors, including green (see *Note* below)
seashell with fine ridges

Note: This new product, available in crafts stores, is noted for the brilliance of its colors, the ease with which it can be worked, and the fact that it dries without baking. When working with Pendo, be sure to keep your hands moist by wiping them on a damp towel. Keep the clay you're *not* working with under glass, as it dries very quickly.

NECKLACE ASSEMBLY

some Pendo clay from above
2 yards ⅛-inch-diameter woven braid in desired color
white resin glue
spray acrylic sealer or clear nail polish

Also: glass or plastic cup (to keep unworked clay covered), toothpicks (for handling leaves and flower parts)

CLAY FLOWERS, BUDS AND LEAVES

1. For 1 pointed petal, roll a small amount of Pendo in the desired color into a ⅜-inch ball. Form the ball into a teardrop shape and then flatten with your finger to make a petal (Diagram A). To add texture to the petal, lightly press one side against the ridged side of a seashell which has been sprayed with acrylic, following the lines in Diagram A. Repeat the step to make approximately 18 to 20 pointed petals.

2. For 1 rounded petal, roll a small amount of Pendo in a second color into a ⅜-inch ball and flatten it with your finger to make a petal (Diagram B). To add texture to the petal, lightly press one side against the ridged side of a seashell which has been sprayed with acrylic, following the lines in Diagram B. Repeat the step to make approximately 10 to 12 rounded petals.

3. For 1 bud, roll a small amount of Pendo in the same color as the rounded petals into a ¼-inch ball. Roll it again to elongate it, as shown in Diagram C, then flatten it and taper one end, as in Diagram D. Roll the piece up tightly to make a bud, rolling from the wider end to the narrower end. Repeat the step to make approximately 16 to 18 buds.

DIAGRAM C   **DIAGRAM D**

4. For 1 leaf, roll a small amount of green Pendo into a ⅜- to ½-inch ball. Proceed as directed for petals, but when adding texture, follow Diagram E. Repeat the step to make approximately 40 to 50 leaves.

5. For flower centers, roll a small amount of green Pendo into 3 balls, each measuring ⅛ inch in diameter.

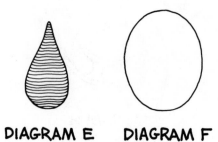

DIAGRAM E   **DIAGRAM F**

6. For 1 flower base, roll a small amount of green Pendo into a ⅝-inch ball and flatten it into the shape of a watermelon, as shown in Diagram F. Repeat the step for a total of 5 flower bases.

DIAGRAM A   **DIAGRAM B**

NECKLACE ASSEMBLY

1. Cut the woven braid in half. Apply glue to ends.

2. For the ends of the necklace, roll a small amount of green Pendo into four ½-inch balls. Form the balls into teardrop shapes, flatten slightly with your finger, then roll each one around one end of cording, as shown in Diagram G.

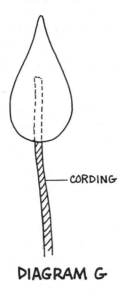

— CORDING

DIAGRAM G

3. Lay the 2 pieces of cording on a flat surface, or pin to a macramé board, to form a necklace. Glue the flower bases to the cording pieces as shown in Diagram H, gluing along the sides of the bases.

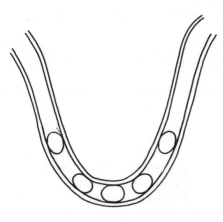

DIAGRAM H

4. Roll up leaves loosely so the textured sides are on the outside. Use a toothpick dipped in glue to pick up and place a number of leaves one by one to each flower base, as shown in Diagram I.

5. Set aside 6 buds, and glue the rest where desired in among the leaves of all the flowers.

6. Following Diagram J, glue the pointed petals to 3 flower bases. Make a circle of Pendo beads and glue to the center of each flower; glue the 3 flower centers to the very center of each circle of beads.

7. Glue the rounded petals to 2 flower bases. In the centers of these flowers, glue the remaining buds that you have set aside and a few Pendo beads.

8. Shape the petals by cupping and curling.

9. Reinforce flowers with more glue.

10. Let the Pendo dry for 12 hours or overnight, then spray with acrylic sealer.

THE CREATIVE TOUCH

For a chunkier necklace, add on more flowers. Or use the flowers in a border for a small dressing table mirror.

DIAGRAM I

DIAGRAM J

131

French Dahlia

This lovely all-beaded arrangement highlights a large dahlia made of a flower center and small petals in one color, surrounded by rings of medium-size and large petals in a complementary color—all attached to a main stem wire. Nine leaves and a bud with small calyx petals are attached to 3 smaller stem wires.

MATERIALS FOR 1 FLOWER, 1 CALYX, 1 BUD AND 9 LEAVES

1 bunch 11° beads in desired color
#28 silver spool wire
1 bunch 11° beads in complementary color
2 bunches 11° beads in green
#28 green spool wire
#32 lacing wire in silver or gold
2-1/3 yards #16 stem wire
green floral tape

Also: small ruler; wire cutters; scissors

PETALS

1. For 1 small petal, string 2 strands of beads in the desired color onto the #28 silver spool wire. Establish a basic row of ¾ inch, and around this wind the beads for a total of 7 rows, rounding both the top and the bottom of the petal. When finished, cut off the bottom loop, leaving only 1 wire; this is to eliminate some bulk when assembling the flower. Repeat the step for 5 more petals, making a total of 6 small petals.

2. For 1 medium-size petal, string 2 strands of beads in the complementary color onto the #28 silver spool wire. Establish a basic row of ⅞ inch, and around this wind the beads for a total of 5 rows, rounding the top of the petal and making a point at the bottom. Repeat the step for 11 more petals, making a total of 12 medium-size petals.

3. For 1 large petal, string 2 strands of beads in the complementary color onto the #28 silver spool wire. Establish a basic row of 1⅛ inches, and around this wind the beads for a total of 5 rows, making a point at the top of the petal and rounding the bottom. Repeat the step for 21 more petals, making a total of 22 large petals.

FLOWER CENTER

For the flower center, string 2 strands of beads in the desired color onto the #28 silver spool wire and make 10 continuous 1-inch loops of beads; when finished, join the first loop to the last by twisting the wires together to secure. Repeat the step, but this time make 12 loops, each measuring 1⅛ inches. Push the wire of the 10-loop unit down through the center of the 12-loop unit and twist both wires together under the flower center.

FLOWER CALYX

For the flower calyx, string 2 strands of green beads onto the #28 green spool wire and make 20 continuous loops of beads, each measuring 2¼ inches; when finished, join the first loop to the last by twisting the wires together to secure. Lace the calyx with #32 lacing wire ½ inch from the top of the loops.

BUD

1. For the bud, string 2 strands of beads in the complementary color onto the #28 silver spool wire and make 10 continuous 1-inch loops of beads; when finished, join the first loop to the last by twisting the wires together to secure. Repeat the step, but this time make 12 loops in the desired color, each measuring 1¼ inches. Push the wire of the 10-loop unit down through the center of the 12-loop unit and twist both wires together under the bud.

2. For 1 calyx petal on the bud, string 2 strands of green beads onto the #28 green spool wire. Establish a basic row of ½ inch, and around this wind the beads for a total of 5 rows, rounding the bottom of the calyx and making a point at the top. Repeat the step for 4 more petals, making a total of 5 calyx petals.

LEAVES

For 1 leaf, string 2 strands of green beads onto the #28 green spool wire. Establish a basic row of ⅝ inch, and around this wind the beads for a total of 13 rows, making a point at the top and the bottom of the leaf. Repeat the step for 8 more leaves, making a total of 9 leaves.

FLOWER ASSEMBLY AND STEM

1. Cut the #16 stem wire into three 15-inch pieces and tape these together with floral tape to make the main stem of the flower. Cut the rest of the #16 stem wire into three 10-inch pieces and one 5-inch piece.

2. Attach the flower center to one end of the main stem with floral tape.

3. Cut a 12-inch piece of the #32 lacing wire. Pull this down through the flower center, then use the lacing wire to attach the small petals one at a time to the flower center, overlapping the petals slightly. Cut away excess lacing wire.

4. Make a ring of the medium-size petals by twisting together 2 of the 3 wires on one petal to 2 of the 3 wires on the next petal, letting the third wire hang down (Diagram A). As you twist the wires tightly together to form the ring, make sure half of each petal overlaps half of the next petal (Diagram B). When all 12 petals are attached, secure the wires of the last petal to the wire ring.

5. Repeat Step 4 for the 22 large petals.

6. Push the ring of medium-size petals up the main stem until it is right under the small petals. Thin out the wires hanging down by cutting on an angle to about 1 inch, as shown by the dotted line in Diagram C. Secure by holding the wires around the main stem and taping with floral tpe.

7. Repeat Step 6 with the ring of large petals.

8. Push the looped flower calyx up the stem until it is right under the large petals. With floral tape, start taping down the main stem, beginning right under the calyx, and tape down 8 inches.

9. With the floral tape, attach 3 leaves to one end of one of the 10-inch pieces of #16 stem wire. Continue taping to the end of the stem. Cut off tape. Repeat the step for the remaining leaves and 10-inch pieces of stem wire.

10. Cut an 18-inch piece of #32 lacing wire. Pull this down through the bud, then use the lacing wire to attach the bud calyx petals one at a time to the bud, overlapping the petals slightly. With floral tape, attach the bud to one end of the 5-inch piece of #16 stem wire. Continue taping to the end of the stem. Cut off tape.

11. At the point where you left off taping the main stem, attach 1 leaf stem to the main stem with floral tape. Tape down the main stem for 1 inch and attach the second leaf stem on the side opposite the first leaf stem. Tape down another inch of the main stem and attach the third leaf stem between first and second leaf stems. Tape down the main stem for another ½ inch to 1 inch and attach the bud stem where desired.

12. Shape the petals by cupping slightly.

VARIATION

The edges of the medium-size and large petals can be the same color as the flower center, but we advise against your attempting this unless you are well acquainted with the craft of beading. To achieve this two-tone effect, cut the spool wire on the fourth row, leaving 6 inches, and feed onto rows four and five 13 beads in the complementary color, 26 beads in the desired color, and 13 beads in the complementary color.

THE CREATIVE TOUCH

For a real decorator's touch, wrap the main flower stem and the leaf and bud stems with ¼-inch-wide velvet ribbon in moss green. Fill your prettiest flowerpot with nonhardening floral clay and place in it a single, stunning dahlia.

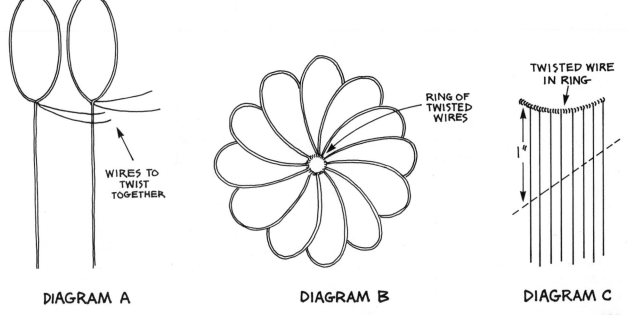

DIAGRAM A   DIAGRAM B   DIAGRAM C

Mod Daisy

A big, bright, cheerful flower, the mod daisy is made of cutout, painted styrofoam pieces trimmed with yarn. The petal unit and smiling flower-center face are glued together, then attached with glue to a dowel-stem inserted into a styrofoam base. Two large styrofoam leaves are secured to the base with toothpicks and glue. Fluffy yarn pompons are attached to the top of the flower and to the base.

MATERIALS FOR 1 FLOWER AND 2 LEAVES

PETAL UNIT

13-inch-square piece styrofoam, 1 inch thick
acrylic paint in desired color

FLOWER CENTER

7-inch-square piece styrofoam, ½ inch thick
acrylic paint in contrasting color to above

LEAVES

two 3 × 8-inch pieces styrofoam, ½ inch thick
acrylic paint in light green

STEM AND BASE

10-inch piece ⅜-inch-diameter dowel
acrylic paint in light green (see above)
8-inch-square piece styrofoam, 2 inches thick
acrylic paint in dark green

FLOWER ASSEMBLY

white resin glue or straight pins
2 yards gift-tie yarn in color to match petal unit
two 3-inch pieces #28 spool wire
1 yard gift-tie yarn in green
2 toothpicks
white resin glue

Also: pencil, compass, tissue paper, scissors; Snow Foam Wonder Cutter™ or sharp serrated knife or X-acto knife; #220 sandpaper; artist's paintbrush, newspaper; black felt-tip marking pen with wide point

PETAL UNIT

1. With a pencil and compass, draw a 12-inch-diameter circle on the 1-inch-thick square of styrofoam. Make a pattern for a petal, tracing from book Pattern 1. With a pencil, very lightly trace the outline

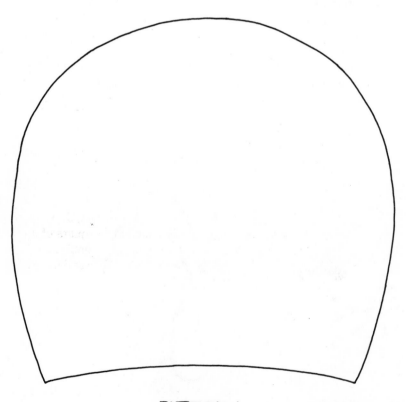

PATTERN 1

of the petal 5 times inside the circle, as shown in Diagram A. Cut the 5-petal unit out of the circle with a knife. Sand the edges lightly until smooth.

2. Paint the petal unit with acrylic paint in desired color. Set aside to dry.

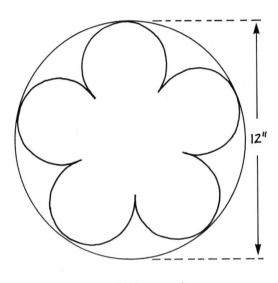

DIAGRAM A

FLOWER CENTER

1. With pencil and compass, draw a 5½-inch-diameter circle on the ½-inch-thick square of styrofoam. Cut out and sand the edges lightly until smooth.

2. Paint the flower center with acrylic paint in the contrasting color. Set aside to dry.

3. With the black felt-tip pen, draw a face on the flower center, as shown in Diagram B.

DIAGRAM B

LEAVES

1. Lightly draw the outline for the leaves on each of the 3 × 8-inch pieces of styrofoam, using the outline in Diagram C as a guide. Cut out each leaf. Sand the edges lightly until smooth.

2. Paint the leaves with light green acrylic paint. Set aside to dry.

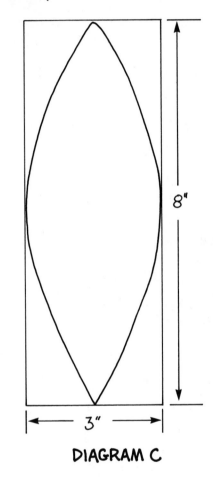

DIAGRAM C

STEM AND BASE

1. Paint the dowel (stem) light green. Set aside to dry.

2. For the base, draw a 7-inch-diameter circle on the 2-inch-thick square of styrofoam. Cut out. Sand the edges lightly until smooth.

3. Paint the base dark green. Set aside to dry.

FLOWER ASSEMBLY

1. Glue the flower center to the middle of the petal unit.

2. Attach the yarn that matches the petals to the edge of the petals and the edge of the flower center, using glue or straight pins. Cut away excess yarn.

3. For 2 pompons, take the yarn left over from Step 2 and cut several 2-inch pieces. Separate the pieces into 2 groups; tie each group of yarn pieces together in the middle with a 3-inch piece of #28 spool wire; fan out the ends of the yarn for a fluffy effect. Attach 1 pompon with glue or a straight pin to the top of the flower, as shown in Diagram D; attach the other with a straight pin to the base in front of the stem.

DIAGRAM D

4. Attach the green yarn to the edge of the leaves, using glue or straight pins.

5. With a pencil, make a hole in the bottom of the flower and in the center of the base, then put a little glue on both ends of the dowel and insert it into the holes.

6. Apply glue to both ends of the toothpicks. Insert one end of a toothpick into the bottom of each leaf, the other end of the toothpick into the base, and push the leaves into the base right beside the dowel.

THE CREATIVE TOUCH

This flower is a perfect table decoration for luncheons, fashion shows and bridge tournaments, or when displayed along the edge of a stage or runway. When making a number of mod daisies, the length of the stems can be varied to make the flowers look as though they were growing in a garden. The mod daisy is also a nice accessory for a little girl's room. Simply follow the directions for the flower, but omit the flower center and glue onto a mirror instead.

We used this rather jolly flower as background to the credits for our 1973 television show "All About Crafts!"

Dollhouse Flowers

A tiny bouquet in a thimble—craft stamens are glued into a styrofoam-filled vase (thimble), the stamen tips then fanned out and arranged. Select the colors for the stamens and thimble to coordinate with your dollhouse décor.

MATERIALS FOR 1 FLORAL ARRANGEMENT

thimble in desired color
tiny piece of styrofoam
12 to 16 double craft stamens in desired color or
    colors
white resin glue

Also: toothpicks, small piece of aluminum foil (for gluing)

ASSEMBLY

1. Fill the thimble with styrofoam and make a hole in the middle of the styrofoam with a toothpick.

2. Fold the stamens in half and dip the folded ends into glue, then push the folded ends into the hole in the styrofoam. Fan out the stamens to form a bouquet.

THE CREATIVE TOUCH

Now that the craze for miniatures is upon us— currently it is the third largest hobby in the world— we would be remiss if we did not include an arrangement that is ideal for people with dollhouses and other types of miniature displays.

Hibiscus

A lavish beaded flower, the hibiscus may take a little more time and patience, but it is well worth the final result. Flower petals, stamens, calyx petals, buds and leaves are all done with beading—the flower parts assembled onto stem wire with floral tape.

MATERIALS FOR 1 FLOWER, 4 BUDS, 4 CALYX PETALS AND 12 LEAVES

2 bunches 11° beads in desired color
#28 silver spool wire
#32 lacing wire in silver or gold
1 strand 11° beads in gold
4 feet #16 stem wire
floral tape to match desired color beads
2 bunches 11° beads in green
#28 green spool wire
green floral tape

Also: small ruler; wire cutters; scissors

FLOWER PETALS

For 1 flower petal, string 3 strands of beads in the desired color onto the #28 silver spool wire. Establish a basic row of ½ inch, and around this wind the beads for a total of 21 rows, rounding the top of the petal and making a point at the bottom. Repeat for 4 more petals, making a total of 5 petals. Lace each petal across the middle with the #32 lacing wire.

STAMENS

1. For 1 stamen, cut a 1½-inch piece of #32 lacing wire and push a single bead in the desired color to the exact center of the wire, then fold the wire in half and twist together to the end (Diagram A). Repeat for 4 more stamens, making a total of 5 stamens.

2. For another kind of flower stamen, repeat Step 2, but this time push 3 gold beads to the center of the wire before folding in half and twisting (Diagram B). Repeat for 29 more stamens, making a total of 30 stamens.

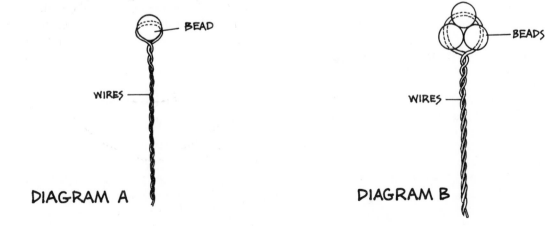

FLOWER CENTER

For the flower center, cut a 6-inch piece of the #16 stem wire and tape it with the floral tape in desired color; then attach the 5 single-beaded stamens to one end with the same floral tape, making sure ½ inch of each stamen wire is left showing. Continue taping down the stem wire with the desired color of tape, and every 1/16 inch attach one of the stamens with gold beads, alternating their placement as you go, and always allowing ½ inch of each stamen wire to show (Diagram C).

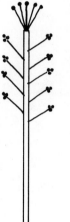

DIAGRAM C

CALYX PETALS

For 1 calyx petal, string 2 strands of green beads onto the #28 green spool wire. Establish a basic row of ½ inch, and around this wind the beads for a total of 5 rows, rounding the bottom of the petal and making a point at the top. Repeat for 3 more petals, making a total of 4 calyx petals.

LEAVES

For each one of the leaves, string 2 strands of green beads onto the #28 green spool wire and establish a basic row of 1 inch. For 2 leaves, wind the beads around the basic row for a total of 13 rows; for 2 leaves, wind the beads for a total of 15 rows; for 4 leaves, wind the beads for a total of 17 rows; and for 4 more leaves, wind the beads for a total of 19 rows. Round the bottom and make a point at the top of each leaf. When finished beading, lace each of the 12 leaves across the middle with #32 lacing wire.

BUDS

1. For 1 small bud petal, string 2 strands of beads in the desired color onto the #28 silver spool wire. Establish a basic row of ½ inch, and around this wind the beads for a total of 11 rows, rounding the top of the petal and making a point at the bottom. Repeat for 3 more petals, making a total of 4 bud petals. Make 1 small bud by folding 2 petals in half lengthwise with the right sides facing out, then interlocking the petals, as shown in Diagram D, and twisting the wires together to secure. Repeat for the second small bud.

TOP VIEW

DIAGRAM D

2. For 1 large bud petal, string 2 strands of beads in the desired color onto the #28 silver spool wire. Establish a basic row of ½ inch, and around this wind the beads for a total of 15 rows, rounding the top of the petal and making a point at the bottom. Repeat for 3 more petals, making a total of 4 bud petals. Make 2 large buds, following directions in Step 1 for small buds.

FLOWER ASSEMBLY AND STEM

1. For the main flower stem, cut two 15-inch pieces of #16 stem wire, tape each piece separately with green floral tape, and then tape the pieces together as one. Set aside.
2. For 1 bud stem, cut one 10-inch piece of #16 stem wire and tape with green floral tape. Set aside.
3. Twist together the wires of the 5 flower petals and fan out the petals so they overlap slightly.
4. Shape the flower petals by cupping slightly and fluting.
5. Push the bottom end of the flower center through the center of the flower petals until 2 inches of the flower center remains above the petals (this would be the part covered with stamens). Secure the flower center below the petals to the petal wires with green floral tape.
6. Attach the 4 calyx petals just underneath the flower petals with green floral tape.
7. Tape down 1 inch of the wires hanging from each of the buds and the leaves with green floral tape,

as shown in Diagram E. As you attach the buds and leaves to the flower, always allow this taped part of the wires to show.

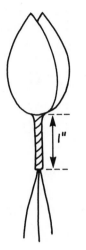

DIAGRAM E

8. Attach the 2 small buds to one end of the main flower stem with green floral tape. Tape down the stem for 5 inches, and as you go, attach the 4 smaller leaves with tape where desired.

9. Attach the flower to the main stem with green floral tape. Tape down 3 more inches of stem, and as you go, attach 3 of the larger leaves where desired.

10. Attach the 2 large buds to one end of the 10-inch piece of #16 stem wire with green floral tape. Tape to the end of the stem wire, and as you go, attach the rest of the leaves with tape where desired. With tape, attach the bud stem to the main flower stem opposite the flower. Tape to the end of the main stem. Cut off tape.

THE CREATIVE TOUCH

One of these beautiful hibiscus in a wine bottle or carafe makes a dramatic, decorative accent for practically any room in either a traditional or contemporary house.

Miniature Iris

This delicate miniature iris is made from a bellcap (a jewelry fixture used on necklaces that fits over the large bead or pearl just before the clasp). Your flower stem is a doubled length of spool wire covered with floral tape. Add 2 slender, tiny leaves cut from a pattern out of soft aluminum. To finish, assemble painted flower and leaves in a pretty container.

MATERIALS FOR 1 FLOWER AND 2 LEAVES

PETALS

½-inch-diameter bellcap (available in crafts stores and jewelry supply houses)

LEAVES

12-ounce soft aluminum can
green acrylic paint

FLOWER ASSEMBLY

8-inch piece #26 spool wire
green floral tape
acrylic paint in desired color
styrofoam block
acrylic paint in contrasting color (optional)
small rhinestone (optional)
white resin glue (optional)
container of your choice

Also: long-nose pliers; scissors, tin snips; pencil, tissue paper; small artist's paintbrush, newspaper

PETALS

For the flower petals, pull down every other section of the bellcap with long-nose pliers, as indicated by the shaded areas in Diagram A.

LEAVES

1. Prepare the aluminum can in the same way you do for the Oriental Poppy in Chapter Seven (page 122). Make your tissue paper pattern for the leaf, tracing from book Pattern 1. Cut 2 leaves out of the aluminum, following Pattern 1.

2. With the small artist's paintbrush, paint the leaves green. Set aside to dry.

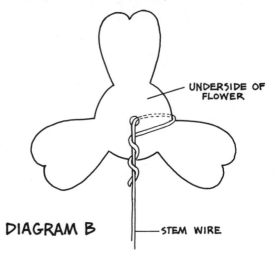

UNDERSIDE OF FLOWER

DIAGRAM B —— STEM WIRE

FLOWER ASSEMBLY

1. Put the #26 spool wire up through the hole in the center of the bellcap, then bring it back to the underside of the flower by bringing it down between 2 petals. Tape the wires together with floral tape, and finish taping to the end of the stem (Diagram B).

2. Holding the flower by the stem, paint it in the desired color. Stick it upright into the block of styrofoam to dry.

3. Highlight the flower with a contrasting color and glue a rhinestone to the center (optional).

4. Insert the broader ends of the leaves into the container of your choice alongside the flower stem.

THE CREATIVE TOUCH

Display several miniature irises and leaves in a suitable container, such as an antique silver saltcellar, by inserting into styrofoam inside the container and covering the top with dried sheet moss.

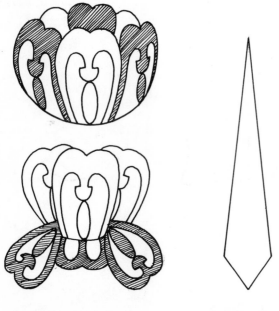

DIAGRAM A   **PATTERN I**

Mountain Flower

The petal units and leaf for the mountain flower are cut from a piece of copper sheeting, following simple patterns. The pieces are then painted and assembled onto stem wire with liquid solder. To make the buds, you dab tiny knobs of liquid solder at random along the flower stem.

MATERIALS FOR 1 FLOWER AND 1 LEAF

PETALS AND LEAF

3 × 4-inch piece copper sheeting
4- to 5-inch piece #18 stem wire (or cut pieces from a thin wire coat hanger)
8- to 10-inch piece #18 stem wire
acrylic paint in desired color
green acrylic paint

FLOWER ASSEMBLY

liquid solder
styrofoam block

Also: pencil, tissue paper, scissors; tin snips, cotton work gloves; ice pick or awl; small artist's paintbrush

PETALS AND LEAF

1. Make tissue paper patterns for the petals and leaf, tracing from book Patterns 1, 2 and 3. With tin snips, cut 2 petal units out of the copper sheeting, following Pattern 1; cut 1 petal unit following Pattern 2; cut 1 leaf following Pattern 3. Wear cotton gloves to protect your hands from the sharp points and edges.
2. Using the tip of the ice pick, vein the leaf.

3. With the ice pick, make a tiny hole in the exact center of each petal unit.
4. Paint the petal units in the desired color. Set aside to dry.
5. Paint the leaf and the pieces of stem wire green. Set aside to dry.

FLOWER ASSEMBLY

1. Put one end of the longer piece of stem wire through the holes in the large petal units and then through the small petal unit, staggering placement of the petals and leaving about ¼ inch of stem wire protruding above the small petal unit. To secure, put a dab of liquid solder between each petal unit and underneath the bottom petal unit right around the hole.
2. For buds, dab 3 or 4 knobs of liquid solder on the flower stem at random. Touch up with green paint when dry.
3. With liquid solder, attach 1 inch of the shorter piece of stem wire to the underside of the leaf, and attach the other end of the wire to the stem of the flower near the base.
4. Shape the small petals by cupping up and inward; shape the large petals by cupping inward slightly.

THE CREATIVE TOUCH

Put a mound of floral clay into the center of a large ashtray in a color that complements the flowers. Insert several of the flowers into the clay and cover the surface with dried moss.

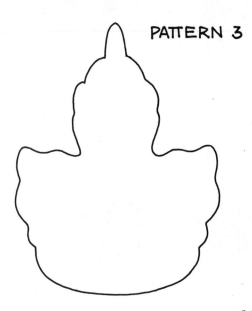

PATTERN 3

PATTERN 2

PATTERN 1

DIAGRAM A   *BASKETWEAVE STITCH*

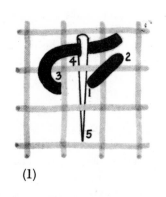

(1)

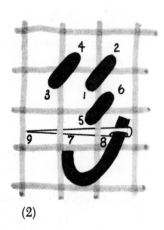

(2)

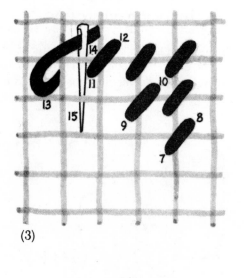

(3)

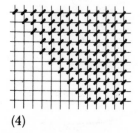

(4)

DIAGRAM B   *CONTINENTAL STITCH*

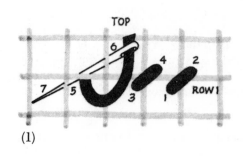

(1)

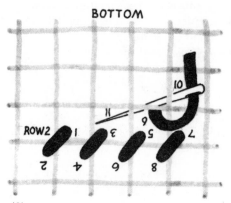

(2)

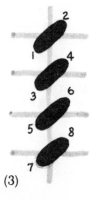

(3)

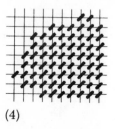

(4)

Needlepoint Flower

Five petals outlined from a pattern are filled in with either a basketweave or Continental stitch, using 2 shades of Persian yarn. The needlepoint petals are wired, backed with felt, then edged with twisted yarn. To complete the flower, petals are wired around craft stamens attached to a long stem wire. Finish the stem with floral tape, taping in 3 craft leaves as you go.

MATERIALS FOR 1 FLOWER AND 3 LEAVES

PETALS

¼-yard piece #18 mono canvas, 40 inches wide
1¼ windings Persian yarn in desired color
½ winding Persian yarn in deeper shade of desired color
#22 needle
white resin glue
#28 white-covered wire
Patricia Nimocks' Super Glue
9 × 12-inch piece felt to match desired color yarn

FLOWER ASSEMBLY AND STEM

cluster single craft stamens in complementary color
12-inch piece #16 stem wire
green floral tape
#28 spool wire
3 large craft leaves
Also: pencil, tissue paper, cardboard; waterproof felt-tip marking pen with fine point; rustproof straight pins, board; scissors; small artist's paintbrush

PETALS

1. Make your tissue paper pattern for the petal unit, tracing from book Pattern 1; cut out a cardboard pattern for the petals, following Pattern 1.

2. Cut the canvas into 2 pieces that are easy to handle; one should be big enough for 2 petals and one big enough for 3. With the marking pen, draw 5 petals on the canvas by outlining the cardboard pattern.

3. Fill in the petals with either the basketweave stitch or the Continental stitch, as shown in Diagrams A and B. You will be using a single thread of yarn in the desired color for most of a petal's area and shading the petal, as indicated in Diagram C, with the yarn in a deeper shade of the desired color.

4. If necessary, block the pieces of canvas by dampening them, pinning them to a board, and pinning the individual petals into the correct shape with rustproof straight pins. Let dry completely.

5. Cut petals from canvas. To prevent raveling, apply white resin glue with a paintbrush to the backs of the petals ¼ inch in from the edge.

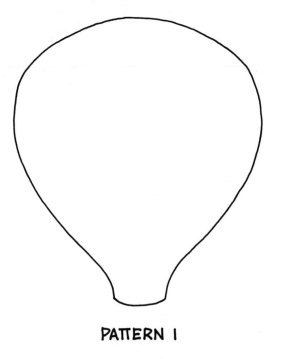

PATTERN 1

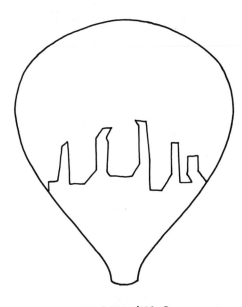

DIAGRAM C

6. Cut five 15-inch pieces of #28 covered wire. Using Super Glue, attach each wire to the back of a petal ½ inch in from the edge, leaving the 2½-inch ends of the wires hanging from the petal base, as shown in Diagram D.

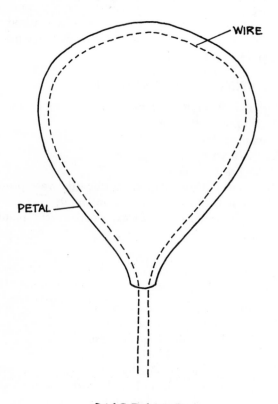

DIAGRAM D

7. Cut 5 petals out of felt following Pattern 1, *except make the petals ⅛ inch larger all around.*

8. Glue the pieces of felt to the backs of the petals with Super Glue.

9. Cut five 16-inch pieces of yarn in the desired color. Knot one end of one of the pieces, hold that end in your left hand, and twist the yarn with your right hand until it is very tight. Fold the twisted yarn in half and pull until taut; the 2 pieces of yarn should automatically twist together, but you can help it along by giving a few twists.

10. With Super Glue and a paintbrush, glue the twisted yarn to the front edge of a petal to cover the felt. Cut away any excess yarn, secure ends with a dot of glue, and dry the petal flat under a suitable weight.

11. Repeat steps 9 and 10 for the 4 remaining petals and pieces of yarn.

FLOWER ASSEMBLY AND STEM

1. Attach the stamen cluster to one end of the #16 stem wire with floral tape.

2. With the #28 spool wire, attach the petals around the stamens one at a time, overlapping the petals slightly, and cover the wire with floral tape. Do not cut off tape.

3. Continue taping down the stem wire for 2 inches, then attach the first leaf with tape. Continue taping down the stem wire for 1 inch, and attach the second leaf opposite the first. Tape down another inch of stem, and attach the third leaf on the same side as the first. Finish taping to the end of the stem. Cut off tape.

THE CREATIVE TOUCH

These striking flowers are equally at home in an antique or contemporary container. The directions can be easily adapted to any shape or kind of flower as long as the flower is not too small.

144

Pussy Willow

Sprigs of pussy willow are made with whole cloves for tiny buds, shaped pieces of chenille stems or pipe cleaners for catkins (pussy willow buds)—all attached with brown floral tape to long stem-wire branches.

MATERIALS FOR 3 BRANCHES

CATKINS (PUSSY WILLOW BUDS)

chenille stems in gray (available in crafts stores), or
   3 pipe cleaners in off-white

BRANCH ASSEMBLY

7 whole cloves with long stems
2 pieces #22 stem wire, each 10 inches long
20-inch piece #18 stem wire
brown floral tape

Also: scissors

CATKINS (PUSSY WILLOW BUDS)

1. For 4 small catkins, cut 1 chenille stem into 4 equal pieces and bend each piece as shown in Diagram A.

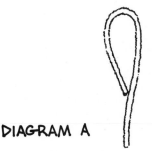

DIAGRAM A

2. For 6 large catkins, cut each of the remaining chenille stems into 3 equal pieces and bend each piece as shown in Diagram B.

DIAGRAM B

BRANCH ASSEMBLY

1. For the buds, tape the cloves to the ends of the pieces of #18 and #22 stem wire with floral tape, distributing the cloves among the 3 wires as desired (Diagram C). Continue taping down each stem wire

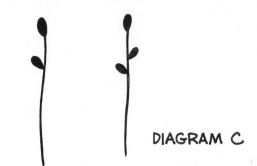

DIAGRAM C

for ½ inch after attaching the last clove to each wire. Do not cut off tape.

2. Continuing with the floral tape, attach the small catkins to the stem wires below the buds, and then attach the large catkins below the small catkins; space catkins ½ inch apart and alternate placement on either side of the stems. Try to tape down each stem wire without cutting off the floral tape until the end.

3. Tape the 3 stems together, as shown in Diagram D.

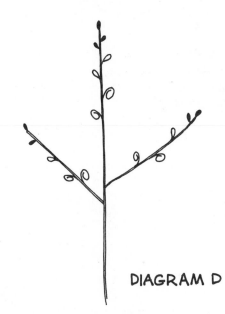

DIAGRAM D

THE CREATIVE TOUCH

Branches of soft pussy willow combine perfectly with the Daffodil and Iris in Chapter Three.

145

PART III

HOW TO USE YOUR FLOWERS

NINE

Flower Arranging

Now that you have learned how to make your flowers, the next step is to learn how to arrange them effectively. This chapter is devoted to our favorite methods of flower arranging, some of which are rather unorthodox.

Many people regard the art of flower arranging as being tricky at best, difficult at worst. But we intend to show you that flower arranging is not only fun and easy to learn, with practice it is also easy to master. And the flowers in this book are easiest of all to arrange, because they will maintain whatever position you put them in.

The skillful flower arranger needs to memorize and master only half a dozen or so simple rules. But it also helps to realize that the rules are not so hard and fast that they can't be broken on occasion, or at least bent a little. If you're pleased with an arrangement, then probably nothing is wrong with it—your eye will tell you when an arrangement is lacking balance or harmony.

1. *Coordinate a flower arrangement with the surrounding design.* A sleekly modernistic arrangement belongs in a contemporary room, not in a period room filled with antiques. Similarly, an old-fashioned nosegay would be at home in many locations, but it would not be appropriate on top of an Oriental chest.

2. *Coordinate the container with the flowers inside it.* The container should be an integral part of the arrangement, but should never vie with the flowers for attention. Unless the container is silver or glass, it should repeat or suggest one of the colors of the flowers.

3. *Strive for pleasing proportions among the flowers, the container, and the location of the arrangement.* In general, flowers above the rim of the container should be 1½ times the container's height—so choose your container with the size of your flowers in mind. And the size of the entire arrangement should be dictated by the location for which it is intended. For example, a single rose in a bud vase looks marvelous on a nightstand, but would look absurd as a dining-table centerpiece. Similarly, a three-foot-high arrangement of gladiolus and snapdragons belongs in a large room like the living room, not in the powder room or kitchen.

4. *The arrangement should be well balanced.* A balanced arrangement will stick out the same distance on both sides of the container, whether or not the arrangement is symmetrical. See Diagram A. Though a balanced arrangement can be heavy at the bottom, it should never be top-heavy, as this is disturbing to the eye. See Diagram B.

5. *Choose flowers for color and texture.* As a general rule, an arrangement should contain no more than two or three kinds of flowers; therefore, you should pay particular attention to color and texture to be assured of an interesting arrangement.

Mix up the flowers so as to play color and texture against one another, but try to keep different flowers of the same color together—if you scatter the colors, you deprive the arrangement of impact. If you exercise care in choosing colors, you can afford a less-than-perfect arrangement in terms of the rest of the design.

6. *An arrangement should have a focal point.* The purpose of a focal point is to draw the eye first to the center of the arrangement, then from the center around and through the rest of it. Usually the focal point is in the lower middle part, and it should always consist of the largest flower, or the flower in the darkest color. As the eye travels to the edges of the arrangement, it should see fewer and smaller flowers. In other words, the middle of the arrangement is dense and heavy while the fringe is light and feathery.

One final word of advice: We always arrange our flowers on a lazy Susan, which enables us to view the arrangement from all sides easily and quickly.

STYLE AND SHAPE OF ARRANGEMENT

The very first thing you have to decide—often even before you make a flower—is whether your arrangement will be in a traditional, contemporary or Oriental style, and whether its shape will be triangular, circular, crescent, S curve, perpendicular or fan.

Traditional arrangements are usually symmetrical and fairly massive, and they convey a feeling of formality. The emphasis here is on the flowers more than on the total effect; in fact, a traditional arrangement will often break the rule of having no more than three kinds of flowers by having a profusion—as many as half a dozen different kinds, with foliage as well.

A contemporary arrangement, in contrast, is sparse and streamlined, playing up the exotic or dramatic

SYMMETRICAL

ASYMMETRICAL

DIAGRAM A

RIGHT

WRONG

DIAGRAM B

features of just a few flowers and their container.

There is a fine line between contemporary and Oriental arrangements, for the latter stress simplicity, too. However, with an Oriental arrangement, you pay more attention to proportion and balance, and you're also restricted to using only certain kinds of Oriental-looking flowers such as fruit blossoms, poppies and irises.

The shape of your arrangement is determined in large part by the kind of flower (or flowers) and the container. Certainly it is essential to decide on a shape before you proceed to shorten or lengthen the stems of flowers or foliage. See Diagram C for the different shapes you may choose.

THE CONTAINER

Containers for artificial flowers can run the gamut from a birdcage to a thimble. Remember, these flowers don't need water, so virtually anything can be put to use as a container. There's no need to stay in the rut of vases and flowerpots—dare to be different and devise containers as interesting as the flowers they hold.

Many fabulous containers are just lying around your house begging to be used. Some good examples: chafing dishes, pitchers, urns, jugs, compotes, tankards, bowls, teapots, kettles, cups and saucers, sugar-and-creamers, coffee mugs, goblets, saltcellars, egg cups, gravy boats, ladles, cheese or pickle crocks, ice buckets, wicker baskets, coal scuttles, lunch pails, sand pails, wicker or metal pocketbooks, hatboxes, wooden boxes, candlesticks and bobeches.

Lots of throwaway items make terrific containers, too—things like tin cans, wine bottles, perfume and other cosmetics bottles.

And don't overlook natural containers such as driftwood, pieces of bark, gourds, a stone, seashells, a coral fan.

These are just a few ideas to get you started—we're positive your imagination will come up with many more.

TOOLS FOR FLOWER ARRANGING

In addition to a container, you need to have at least some of the following items on hand before you begin putting your flower arrangement together: styrofoam, Oasis, nonhardening floral clay, floral adhesive, dried sheet moss, stem wire, spool wire, wire cutters, floral tape, floral picks, toothpicks, matchsticks, plaster of Paris, clear plastic lids from food containers, ribbon.

Styrofoam inside the container works well for a majority of arrangements—naturally you'll want to cover it up with dried moss. For heavy flowers, such as those made with beads, fill the container with nonhardening floral clay or plaster of Paris. Tall and bulky flowers should be embedded in plaster of Paris. If you are combining artificial flowers with real flowers or foliage, keep the latter fresh by putting Oasis inside the container.

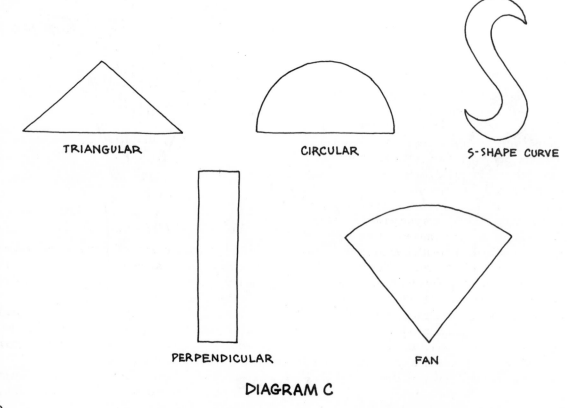

TRIANGULAR   CIRCULAR   S-SHAPE CURVE

PERPENDICULAR   FAN

DIAGRAM C

FAKING A WATERLINE

If your container is glass or crystal, you may want it to look as though the flowers are actually standing in water. Take a plastic lid from a food container and trim off the edge to fit the inside circumference of the container, then with an ice pick or awl, punch as many holes in the lid as you need for stems. Push the lid into the container to where one would expect a waterline, and insert the flower stems through the holes. See Diagram D.

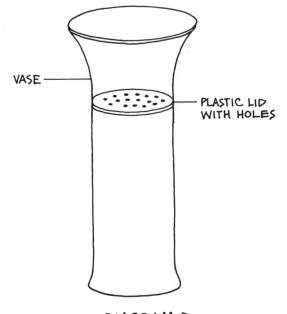

VASE

PLASTIC LID WITH HOLES

DIAGRAM D

FILLER FLOWERS

These are the flowers or other plant material you include in your arrangement in addition to your artificial flowers. There are several reasons for filler flowers. Sometimes an arrangement would look too heavy without breaking it up with fillers—for example, our rich and heavy anemones are combined with two fillers: dried baby's breath and cut fern. Another reason for filler flowers is to act as a backdrop for showing off the flowers you wish to highlight —a good example is our arrangement of cabbage roses, where dried baby's breath is used so skillfully as to create a picture of each rose. Filler flowers are often used when you only have time and energy to create a very few permanent flowers—in such cases, the fillers literally fill out the arrangement and help a few fabulous artificial flowers go a long way. Finally, filler flowers can be employed to create a special, perhaps startling, effect, as when we combine poppies made of aluminum cans with dried eucalyptus leaves.

Our very favorite filler flowers are baby's breath, statice and heather. Other excellent fillers are Queen Anne's lace, thistle, goldenrod, milk pods and pampas grass. Though filler flowers can be purchased inexpensively at crafts stores and florist shops, you can grow your own or pick them along country roads and dry them at home.

Drying filler flowers: The method we use is called air-drying, and it couldn't be simpler. Pick the flowers when they're in their prime, and pick them in the heat of the day when they have as little moisture in them as possible. Tie them up in small bunches inside brown paper bags and hang them upside down in a warm location for two weeks. See Diagram E.

When the flowers are completely dry, spray them with acrylic sealer or, for a special effect, with acrylic paint in a matte finish.

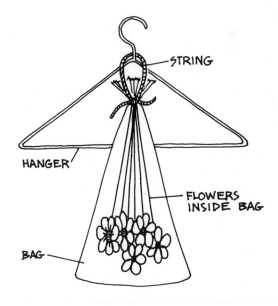

STRING

HANGER

FLOWERS INSIDE BAG

BAG

DIAGRAM E

CARING FOR ARTIFICIAL FLOWERS

With proper care, all the flowers in this book will last for many years. Keeping them free of dust and grime is the primary task, and here is how to go about it with the different types.

Fabric flowers can be sprayed with Scotchgard™ to make them almost impervious to grease and dust, a procedure we strongly endorse if the flowers are to be displayed in or near the kitchen.

When fabric or paper flowers get dusty, they can be cleaned quickly and easily with a hand-held hair dryer set at "cool" on the lowest possible speed—a once-over-lightly sweep is sufficient. Paper flowers can also be cleaned with a feather duster. Or, if they are particularly dirty, shake them in a paper or plastic bag filled with half a cup of sand or kosher salt.

Plastic flowers are cleaned by immersing them completely in soapy water, then rinsing off the soap and drying them outdoors in the shade.

Individual beaded flowers can be cleaned by dunking them quickly into cool water to which a few drops of ammonia has been added. Then wipe them dry with paper towels. Whole arrangements of beaded flowers are best cleaned with an aerosol chandelier cleaner.

Fabric flowers often need reshaping after a spell of humid weather (it causes them to wilt) or after being packed away for a while. Usually they can be revived satisfactorily by holding them over a steaming teakettle, after which they should be given a light coat of spray starch. If the flowers are still floppy, spray them lightly with crystal-clear acrylic sealer. (*Note:* If you live near the water, use only the acrylic sealer instead of starch, because starch isn't effective in areas of excessive humidity.) Never use hair spray; the flowers will stay tacky!

When a flower has been sprayed with starch so many times over the years that it practically *is* starch, you should spray it with a heavy coat of the clear acrylic sealer and hang it upside down to dry. We finally had to do this with our shaggy zinnias, and today the arrangement is almost as beautiful as it was ten years ago—furthermore, the flowers are now practically impervious to humidity. The only disadvantage to using acrylic sealer is that they make the flowers feel stiff to the touch.

One of the best ways to keep your flowers clean and fresh looking is to change them often. Just as you'd constantly change the location and arrangements of real flowers, so should you try placing your artificial flowers in different locations throughout the house and recombining them with other flowers in new arrangements.

You can also prolong the life of your flowers by simply packing them away for periods of time. The best storage for individual flowers is a large, flat dress box. Or, if you don't want to disassemble an entire arrangement, cover it with a large plastic bag—if you blow some air into it before sealing, the plastic stays off the flowers, and you won't have to reshape them later.

TEN

Decorating with Your Flowers

If a poll were taken of leading interior designers asking their opinion as to the most important finishing touch in a room, we bet most of them would say plants and flowers. So, now that you've learned how to make and arrange your flowers, here comes the final step: where and when to use them for maximum effect.

PLACING THE ARRANGEMENT

When a floral arrangement will back up against a wall, you must consider what is on that wall. If the wall is covered with wallpaper in a floral pattern in several colors, you should not attempt to duplicate those colors in your arrangement or it will simply fade into the background. Instead, pick up just one or two of the wallpaper colors, probably the weaker ones.

The texture of the wall is also a consideration. If it is covered with grass cloth or a similarly rough texture, you'd be smart not to put burlap flowers in front, because the two textures are too much alike. On the other hand, silk or beaded flowers are lovely against a rough or nubby wall.

If your wall is busily patterned or vibrantly colored and competes too much with your floral arrangements, consider hanging a mirror behind the arrangement—this sets off flowers from their background most effectively. If you don't want to hang a mirror, you'll have to avoid putting multi-colored arrangements against the wall, reserving them instead for spots in the middle of the room.

If there's enough space on the table (or other surface), consider grouping your arrangement with a piece of sculpture or bric-a-brac. Obviously, whatever you choose must complement the arrangement in color, theme or style, and scale.

COLOR, SIZE AND STYLE

These three components of a floral arrangement determine the room or location in which it belongs. Rooms decorated in pale or neutral colors invite arrangements of brightly colored flowers. Our pompons and Oriental poppies, for example, would provide welcome notes of color to otherwise subdued surroundings. On the other hand, in bright or outstandingly patterned rooms, restrict your floral arrangements to white or neutral shades, or to one or two colors matching the room's colors. Our seashell bouquet and arrangement of white petunias in a fireplace grate are perfect for rooms with lots of competing color and pattern.

It isn't so much the size of the room that you have to watch out for as the space immediately around the arrangement and the size of the furniture on which it sits. Don't let the arrangement overwhelm its surroundings—nor, conversely, should it become lost in a cavernous area.

Actually you can have a large arrangement in a small room if other factors are favorable. Take a small foyer, for example. Here a generous-size bouquet could sit on a table if the table top is fairly big, and, better yet, if there's a mirror behind it to give the illusion of a larger room. Or the arrangement could sit on the floor in a corner, providing it doesn't interfere with traffic.

Color and size will be greater variables than will style, for the simple reason that your house already has a certain style—it's up to you to follow through by making flowers and arrangements to suit that style, whether it be early American, French provincial, Danish modern or whatever.

FLOWERS IN THE HOME

Upstairs, downstairs, inside and out, there's virtually no nook or cranny in a house or apartment that doesn't benefit from being decked with flowers. What we urge you to do is to stand in each room in your own home and study it carefully. Where are the bare places? Where are the dull spots? What kinds of floral arrangements would fill up the space or brighten the appearance?

THE FRONT DOOR

There are few sights more cheery than a basket of flowers hanging on the front door—they speak a welcome to arriving guests and suggest a contented family inside. Residents of one block in our town have agreed to keep flowers or other plant material hanging on their doors, and they change them four times a year according to season. That block is a pleasure to everyone.

It is best to use plastic flowers on a front door, unless you live in a mild climate or have a storm door for protection. In Chapter Seven we tell how to transform the lowly five-and-ten variety of plastic flower to a thing of beauty.

HALLS AND ENTRYWAYS

Flowers in a front hall or foyer provide guests with a good first and last impression of your home and contribute a necessary note of sunshine to other halls in the house. Most halls are sadly lacking in color or other eye-catching detail, so this is where you should use bright floral arrangements, such as ours of powder puffs and cabbage roses.

Large arrangements can go on the floor in a bare corner or at the foot of an open stairway or stairwell. Medium-size and small arrangements probably look best on a table or commode. The drama of a beautiful floral arrangement is lost unless it is well lighted, and since many halls are notoriously dark, we urge you to correct the lighting situation—perhaps by installing a spotlight or two.

THE LIVING ROOM

More than any other room in the house, the living room offers endless possibilities for the display of floral arrangements, and we hope you won't stop at just one or two. The living room is where you do most of your entertaining—sometimes it's the only room a guest sees—so you want to put your best foot forward here, and what better way than with bouquets strategically placed to complement or carry out the room's color scheme.

Some obvious areas for floral arrangements are the coffee table, fireplace mantel or hearth, end tables and occasional tables, stereo console, and, if there is one, a desk. But wherever you put them, make sure the arrangements are in scale with the surroundings—an arrangement on the coffee table, for example, shouldn't be so tall that people have to peer around it when conversing. And of course they should harmonize with the furnishings and the colors. Use your most impressive containers in the living room, too, where they will be admired by one and all.

THE DINING ROOM

This is where you'll also want flowers the year round. However, your choice of places for flowers here is usually limited to the dining table and some kind of buffet or sideboard, though some dining rooms also contain serving carts, china cupboards or a hutch.

The floral centerpiece (including the candlesticks), for the dining table should not occupy more than a third of the surface, and the candles should be no more than ten inches high, so that diners can see over them. Arrange the centerpiece so it's attractive when viewed from all sides, and be sure to use a handsome container, since it won't be much below eye level when people are seated. While the colors in the centerpiece do not always have to match the china and linens, they should at least be complementary.

Because dining room furniture is limited and usually lacks the bold and extensive splashes of color you get in upholstered furniture elsewhere in the house, you can rely on floral arrangements to supply the room with color and give it life and focus. A buffet or sideboard is a great spot for a colorful bouquet, and, unless there's a mirror behind it, you don't have to worry about arranging the back of the bouquet, which also means you need fewer flowers for it.

Sometimes when we have a lot of guests for a special occasion, we push the dining table to the side of the room and set up card tables. These we cover with sheets in pretty pastels, and in the center we put small matching floral arrangements. Or, if guests can all be seated around the dining table, we might make individual floral centerpieces for each guest to take home as a memento.

THE FAMILY ROOM OR DEN

Most families we know watch television in a family room or den, and we can think of no single piece more in need of beautifying with flowers than the TV set. Many family rooms are paneled with wood and tend to be dark, so your best bet may be brightly colored flowers with textures that go well with wood. Your arrangement will probably be only three-sided, as most TV sets back up to the wall. Other places in the family room for flowers are tables and desks, a piano, an empty fireplace grate in the summertime, and bookshelves where small floral arrangements can break the monotony of rows of books.

BEDROOM AND BATH

Though most surfaces in these rooms are covered with cosmetics bottles, jewelry boxes, framed snapshots, alarm clocks and the like, you should be able to find a spot for a small floral arrangement in one or two accent colors. Many bathrooms in newer homes have twin sinks set in a sweeping vanity top, and here a splash of color would be most welcome.

Other places for flowers would be on a shelf that holds fancy powders, lotions and bubble baths, or on the water container behind the toilet. And remember that guest bedrooms and powder rooms receive very little wear and tear, so there's every reason to create floral arrangements as the finishing touch.

THE KITCHEN

There are few places in kitchens for floral arrangements, but because we believe that every room deserves flowers, here are some suggestions for where to put them: on top of a kitchen cabinet near the ceiling; on the windowsill over the sink; at the end of a long counter; on top of the refrigerator; in the middle of a breakfast table.

Since kitchen surfaces collect dust and grease, any flowers you make for the room must be able to withstand frequent washing or wiping.

FLOWERS IN THE OFFICE

Artificial flowers are extremely well suited to a reception room or inner office. Not only do they often have too little light for real plants and flowers, but people in offices don't really have time to water, fertilize, pinch back and repot blooming plants. So we're in favor of creating artificial floral arrangements to liven up the atmosphere—certainly customers and clients are bound to respond with pleasure.

The best place in a reception room for a floral arrangement is probably the table on which magazines are displayed. If the receptionist doesn't double as a hard-working secretary, a small bouquet could decorate this desk, too. (This isn't true inside an office—here a floral arrangement would add unnecessary clutter.)

Other places for flowers include tables, bookshelves, or on the deep windowsills office buildings often have. Finally, don't overlook meeting rooms and board rooms where the conference table, typically looking like a shiny brown pond, can be considerably dressed up with an appropriate floral centerpiece.

Keep floral arrangements for office environments fairly simple and streamlined like the décor itself, unless the office has been designed with an earlier period in mind.

FLOWERS IN CHURCH

The recent escalation in prices of fresh-cut floral arrangements has made it impossible for all but the wealthiest churches to keep fresh flowers in the sanctuary every day of the year, or even every Sunday, for that matter. But for centuries, flowers have been used to enhance church altars and vestibules, and since we are loathe to see a lovely custom in jeopardy, we recommend that churches consider artificial floral arrangements. Planning and making such arrangements would be a wonderful project for church auxiliary groups.

Floral arrangements for a church sanctuary are handled differently from those at home. For one thing, they will probably be quite large, because they'll exist in a vast space with little or no furniture around except altar and pews. For this reason, we strongly advise creating arrangements right on the spot—not at home or in the church basement.

Also, because of the presence of multi-colored, stained-glass windows, we think the flowers should not attempt to duplicate or complement the windows, but rather should be seasonal. And we recommend flowers made out of silk because they tend to be the most realistic in appearance. Choose plain containers, avoiding the elaborate urns usually associated with churches, and keep the overall arrangement simple but full.

We hope we have given you dozens of sound ideas for incorporating many kinds of artificial flowers into the design of your home. So now we encourage you to get to work and start creating your favorite blossoms. Remember that the more floral arrangements you make, the more often you'll be able to change them.

And don't forget floral arrangements for the holidays. Here you don't have to be too concerned with keying them to your color scheme and style, for it's the theme of the holiday that matters. But don't think you always have to be traditional either; be inventive. One of our pet Christmas wreaths, for example, is the handsome artichoke wreath in Chapter Six, and we've seen a simply stunning wreath made with hay and trim and the Cornhusk Flower in Chapter Seven. Or, instead of the usual dyed eggs at Easter time, consider the more contemporary arrangement of Forget-Me-Nots and plain eggs in Chapter Seven. And at Thanksgiving, what better way to give thanks than with a centerpiece made with cornhusks and loaves of bread, as featured in Chapter Seven.

Whether decorating your home for the holidays or every day, we think you'll find it a delightful, easy and rewarding job when you count on the flowers in this book to help you out. Once you get hooked, flower-making is a hobby that stays with you forever—just like the flowers.

Index